Becoming
Magick

Becoming Magick

New & Revised Magicks for the New Aeon

By David Rankine

Published by
Mandrake of Oxford
PO Box 250
OXFORD
OX1 1AP (UK)

A CIP catalogue record for this book is available from the British Library and the US Library of Congress.

ISBN 1869928-814

Contents

Acknowledgements

I would like to thank the following people for their assistance, direct or indirect, over the years:

Sorita, my Shakti, for inspiring me and being my Muse, and for helping me put together my ideas on much of the material. Love Never Dies.

Graham Jebbett (aka Grey Fox), for testing out material and working with me over the last eighteen years as a magickal colleague and friend.

Jenny Sumaya for the front cover photograph. Inbaal, for her help and ideas with the analysis of the Hebrew letters. Brian Andrews, for drawing the Mudra pictures, and his scanner! Ian Read, for being the first person to publish my writings as Jack Dracula in *Chaos International*; it is a grace to find men so honourable in this world.

This book is dedicated to the Great Goddess Maat

May Her Truth and Balance fill all who seek Wisdom

Introduction

This book contains material that is the result of many years of working with different systems and techniques, and eclectically creating my own system. The system I have created incorporates elements from diverse sources, and is (obviously) eminently workable. For me one of the driving motivations of magick is to discover the unknown and push the boundaries of existing knowledge and practice.

Readers may find themselves disagreeing with some of the ideas or techniques given, which is fine. The material presented henceforth is for integration or dismissal as appropriate into your system of practice. I hope that the range of techniques and information I have combined will encourage the reader to re-examine some of their perceptions.

If you find yourself recognizing parts of the material in this book, it is probably because some of it has been published or part-published in various magickal journals and magazines in the last twelve years under my pseudonym of Jack Dracula.

David Rankine

I do not believe in taking on board and using complete systems of practice (obviously symbol systems such as Qabalah have great value in training and as tools), and feel the excessive parrot fashion use of Aleister Crowley's material is one of the great tragedies of modern magick.

Precision is an essential quality for a magician to have, and this extends to the research done around a subject you work with. For this reason you may notice some differences between material I have presented and the way it is often portrayed.

To practice the material in this book you will require a basic level of competence in meditation, visualization, pranayama, bodywork, mantra and invocation. I will only discuss these topics where material presented differs from common forms, or to illustrate specific ideas, in an attempt to save the reader from repetition or insult to the intelligence.

Control of the mind, the imagination, the body and the voice can be considered the cornerstones of magickal growth. Without working hard at these areas, through such techniques, you will always be building on sand and never develop the firm foundations necessary for fulfillment of your potential and realisation of your genius.

My own perception of deity is that they exist outside us as well as inside, and this is reflected in the material in some places. This book does not set out to discuss the nature of deity; however it is inevitable that, as with the Hermetic maxim "as above, so below", they should be found in the text. Many people have argued the nature of deity in recent years, and this is largely irrelevant to much of the material herein. However my perception is that devotional work to deities opens you up

10

to a more complete perception of the world, and facilitates mystical experience as an ongoing part of daily life.

I hope that some of the material in this book may cause you to either question what you have been told is standard practice, or to violently disagree and reaffirm strongly your own views. Like other magickal methods, the examination of taboos and the relevance of keeping or breaking them can be very powerful.

Through writing this book I have strived to express techniques and, to an extent, philosophies, that I have developed over a period of about twenty years of experimenting. To this end this work is an expression of my will as the word, a realisation of force in form. I can do no more than end with André Padoux's definition of Tantra which sums up my feelings about the personal practice of magick as a process of achieving perfection.

"(Tantra) is an attempt to place desire, in every sense of the word, in the service of liberation … not to sacrifice this world for liberation's sake, but to reinstate it, in varying ways, within the perspective of salvation. This use of desire and of all aspects of this world to gain both worldly and supernatural enjoyments and powers, and to obtain liberation in this life, implies a particular attitude on the part of the (Tantric) adept towards the cosmos, whereby he feels integrated within an all-embracing system of micro-macrocosmic correlations."

David Rankine

1 What is Magick & How Does It Work?

What is magick? Avoiding the popular definitions given in some books, I suggest that magick is consciously directed energy flowing towards evolution. By extension, magickal techniques can be seen as practical ways of creating positive change in the self and the environment (which of course includes people and animals). A vital factor in the resurgence of currently practiced pagan religions is that they contain, in differing amounts, three strands, those of magick, mysticism and religion.

If we consider mysticism to be personal revelatory experience of the immanent and transcendent, and religion to be the social context for understanding and integrating these experiences, then magick can also be seen as a bridge between the self and the environment, and a way to induce revelatory experiences.

The importance of using magickal technique as part of one's spirituality is that it enables the certainty of direct experience by providing the opportunities for personal mystical experience at many levels, rather than relying on faith. This enables each seeker to experience for themselves and create their own personal style, working the magick that is best suited to their own unique spirituality and path. This element of direct experience resulting from a dynamic spiritual life ensures we have responsibility for our own growth and actions – we have to dare to grow!

Many authors and groups assume things are already known – like how does magick work? The longer I practice magick, the more I feel that magick is not complex, as many people like to make out for a variety of reasons, rather magick is so simple as to be beyond complete understanding. Consideration of how magick works has led me to conclude that at the end of the day there is one basic principle in magick, which can perhaps most easily be considered from two slightly different perspectives.

The Unity of Diversity

This perspective embodies the hermetic axiom of "As above, so below", that man (as the microcosm) is a reflection of the universe (macrocosm), and that all of existence is part of the same whole. This idea may be found in most systems, from the interconnected threads of the web of Wyrd and the "Eagle" in Castaneda's writing to the Tao and the Goddess who is all that is and was and ever shall be. I perceive the Egyptian Goddess Maat to be the best depiction of this – as Truth and natural order She is the balance of perfection we strive to embody and radiate.

This principle of interconnectedness contains the basic essence of sympathetic magick, that as all things are connected they may exert an influence on one another irrespective of distance, and the link is stronger when there has been a bond or proximity (such as hair, nails, body fluids, personal possessions, etc).

To further consider the idea of man as the reflection of the universe, if we consider the universe to comprise of energy manifesting at different levels of consciousness, then the nature of the energy in the universe is also reflected in man. We use about 10% of our brains in the conscious mind, the remainder being the unconscious and governing the involuntary functions of the body (like breathing). The universe likewise is comprised of about 10% matter, and 90% dark matter. Dark matter is still largely a mystery to scientists, in the same way as the unconscious is a mystery to man. As scientists seek to learn about dark matter and create a theory of unified forces, so magicians seek to learn about the unconscious and develop a unified consciousness.

The hermetic perspective, like many others in magick, is now gaining acceptance in quantum physics (i.e. two particles which have interacted can continue to exert influence on each other irrespective of distance). This principle has implications for all spiritual seekers, implying that anything we do to the universe we do to ourselves, and that experiences of oneness with the universe ("samadhi", "nirvana", etc) are attainable through any approach that acknowledges this. Consideration of this principle can open up a cornucopia of symbols to gain greater understanding e.g. on a cosmic level we can literally interpret the Orphic oath "I am a child of earth and starry heaven", as the fact that we are made of the same stuff as the stars, though the molecules may have been through many millions of transitions and interactions in-between.

The Doctrine of Signatures

This perspective accords that all things being connected, there are relationships between the differing energies and forms, such that some resonate with one another and may be used to influence others or attract a particular form of energy. The practice of using ritual tools, colour and symbolic correspondences and power objects can be seen as an expression of this perspective, as can such techniques as trance dance, mask work, invocation and drawing down.

Symbols as an expression of the mysteries of energy and form transcending the limitations of language are perhaps the best example of the power inherent in these linkages which may be drawn upon even though they can not be fully expressed or understood. This is an expression of the ecological principle - everything is connected to everything else.

So although magickal systems may seem complex or unwieldy, what matters of course is the flow of energy through it, and if we see the simplicity involved, we can better appreciate the beauty of existence and learn from it and grow. If it works for you then do it, use the techniques which work well, find a good banishing, energising, etc.

A practical example of the simplicity of magick and how to appreciate it is in the way we experience our senses. As a species we are largely trained to take our major cues from our vision. Try regularly walking around your home blindfolded, and you will soon become more focused on your memory and sense of proximity. When you can do this with ease, try doing the same on all fours. Then when that is easy, try and find a space where you can repeat this, but where the mental map is not so clear, like a willing friend's space. This may seem a little silly, but is actually a very practical way of encouraging the conscious mind to focus more on input from the other, non-visual senses.

We need to listen to the messages of all of our senses. Not for nothing is smell known as the evoker of memory, for example. As magick expands our mental perceptions and boundaries, so we can train our consciousness to expand its sensory input to enable us to pick up the subtler signs and cues in our environment.

To seriously practice magick we need to harness and enhance the gifts we have. Specifically the mind, the voice and the body. Addressing these in turn, to enhance the power of our minds we practice meditation, concentration and visualization exercises, etc to strengthen these abilities and develop our willpower and mental fortitude. Our voices produce sound, which is transmutable energy, so the more we practice using our voices, and train them to be able to intone and project sound, the higher the energies we can raise through their use.

Another important aspect of magickal development is the release and integration of energy held trapped in body armour, a term coined by the brilliant psychologist Wilhelm Reich. Reich's writings address, both directly and indirectly, a lot of issues and ideas of great relevance to the magician, and I cannot recommend his writings strongly enough. Body armour, according to Reich, is the stress, tension and emotional trauma we store physically in our muscles, producing not only aches and pains, but also encouraging a rigid and fixed perception of the world without the panoramic view the magician seeks.

Many people seem to end up ignoring the physical when they start practicing magick. But the physical is the plane that we are generally trying to achieve our effects on, so the more balanced our physical life is, both in the sense of having a healthy body (through good diet and practicing body work such as massage, yoga, tai chi, qi gong, martial arts etc) and having a stable material base, the more able we become to realise the intent of our magicks. Developing magickal ability could be likened to the structure of a pyramid, you have to put huge amounts of work in the focus, concentration and discipline of doing the basic daily exercises. To be an adept; accomplishing the altered states that correspond to the view from the top of that pyramid, first make sure your life is in order.

A danger that can arise from magickal work is inflation of the ego, an extremely common and insidious occurrence which can be one of our greatest hindrances. Again, working on perception and perspective can help here. Rather than getting into a mindset which says "I am better than all these 'normal' people with their mundane lives who don't do rituals and have no meaning in their existence", instead accept that everyone is different, and on their own path, which may not involve a strong spiritual component. There can be no competition with someone on a different path, we are all treading our own paths of self-realisation, and trying to compete or be boastful or superior shows a lack of grace and balance, not an advanced adept!

2   The Importance of Maat

The goddess Maat is a figure of central importance to Egyptian magick. For me, Her significance is undiminished by the passing of time, and I perceive Her as being of utmost importance and relevance to the magick of today. For anyone following the doctrine of Thelema, of finding and pursuing the true will, which is an alignment with harmony and pursuit of truth, I see Maat as the key figure.

Maat in Ancient Egypt

Maat embodied the concepts of truth, justice and cosmic order. She is mentioned in the *Pyramid Texts* as standing behind Ra, implying that She is the source of his power. As time passed She became seen as the daughter of Ra, and also as the wife of Thoth, God of Magick. Maat was also sometimes partnered (though not as wife) with Heka, the embodiment of magick.

She was usually shown as a beautiful young woman with wings and Her symbol of the white ostrich feather on Her head. The feather implies air and the breath of life, implicit in terms found in ancient Egyptian texts like "breathing in Maat". The term "upholding Maat" was sometimes used to describe the practice of magick.

Maat was seen to have several major roles in the continued well-being of Gods and men. One of her symbols was a hieroglyph of the plinth on which statues stood. This implies the supremacy of Maat in representing the order that even the gods strive to perceive. This may be seen through Maat shrines usually being present in the temples of other gods rather than being distinct, and also statements like "the gods live on Maat" (cf the statue plinth).

The most significant role of the Pharaoh was to uphold Maat, and the success of his reign would be measured by how well he did this. Many of the Pharaohs took the title "beloved of Maat" to emphasise their position.

One of the most important ceremonies performed by the Pharaoh was the presentation of Maat, where he would make a ritual presentation of a Maat statue in the Temple of the Gods, saying "I give you Maat with my left hand, my right hand protecting her". The presentation was most often made to creator gods, like Amun, Ra and Ptah.

As the goddess of justice Maat was the patron of judges, who wore small gold pendants of Her as a sign of their authority. Depictions of Maat as Her anthropomorphic form or a feather were also sometimes painted onto their tongues with magickal ink by magicians to demonstrate they spoke only words of truth when performing their spells.

In Her role of goddess of the balance in the underworld, Maat was the central figure of this rite of passage. Her feather of truth is weighed on the scales against the heart, and She also presides over the weighing with Osiris in His role as Lord of the Underworld. The weighing took place in the Hall of Two Truths, and Maat was often depicted in twin form here. The gods who act as the judges of the divine tribunal of the soul are called the "Council of Maat".

The soul of the deceased had to recite the negative confessions, forty-two statements of good conduct which were seen as guidelines to living a balanced life, a life of Maat. If the heart of the deceased then balanced against the feather, the deceased was judged to be "true of heart and voice" and would live with the gods. If not they were fed to the devourer of souls and annihilated. There is a parallel between the forty-two pylons or portals to be passed through on the journey to the Hall of Two Truths, corresponding in number to the negative confessions that had to be made.

Historically it is interesting to note that when Akhenaten replaced the worship of the gods with the monotheistic worship of the Aten, the sun-disk, the one deity he maintained was Maat. He described himself as "living in truth" (Maat). Even with his revolutionary ideas Akhenaten still recognised the need for truth and cosmic balance.

Maat had a variety of titles, which emphasise Her roles in the ancient Egyptian cosmology. These epithets include:

- Directress of the Underworld.
- Justice.
- Lady of the Hall of Judgment.
- Lady of the Heavens Queen of Earth.

- Law.
- Maat the Beautiful.
- Perfect Measure.
- Right Order.
- Sustainer of the Sun.
- The Changeless.
- The Good Gift.
- The Undeviating.
- That which Is True.
- Tracer of the Course of the Sun.
- Truth.
- Twofold Truth.
- The Measure of the Heart.

A standard principle of magickal work with deity is "invoke often". This should perhaps be extended to "invoke often, align often", to ensure one is following the optimum path, as directed by your true will. To this end I have included a short Maat devotion I created for daily practice. The specifics of the practice are up to the individual. I would merely recommend a statue and/or image of Maat on the altar, as well as a white feather. Other details are optional and a matter of personal preference.

Maat Devotion

My sword is my will, true of intent
My will is of Maat, my purpose unbent

I strive for perfection
In thought and in deeds
In grace and in beauty
To nurture the seeds

To balance the feather
I must focus and shine
So magick and truth
Will always be mine

I honour great Maat
And recount my actions:

I have not lied
I have not cheated
I have not killed
I have not knowingly harmed
I have not broken my word

I have acted with love
I have acted with compassion
I have acted with will
I have acted with honour
I have acted with Truth

I seek to always perform my true will and to strive ever for
perfection in all things

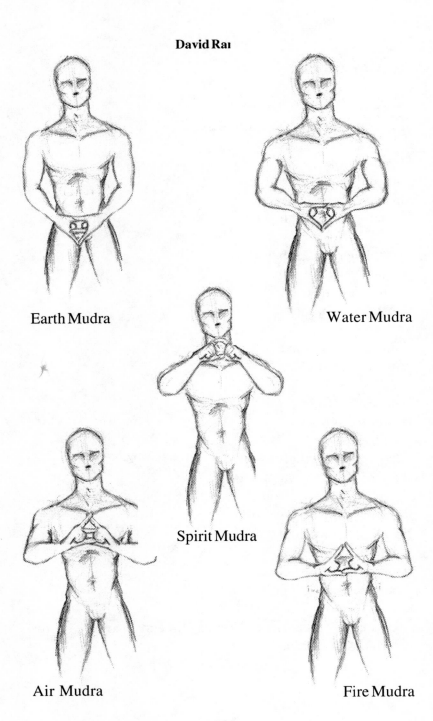

Earth Mudra

Water Mudra

Spirit Mudra

Air Mudra

Fire Mudra

3   A Ritual Opening

I strongly emphasise the use of the voice in magick, sound being transmutable energy. The use of words of power, whatever their language, is of great benefit in ritual, exalting the consciousness by their essence and sound. To this end, I present a ritual opening I developed for use to begin the creation of the magickal sphere.

From this opening one would move into a standard banishing or using words of power to create a sphere, or further empower the temple if you have one permanently set up. If desired you could turn to the quarters when saying the lines for the elements and making the gestures, though personally I tend to face my main central altar when doing it.

Emmi gas vios kai ouranou asteroentos

Let earth be still   *Make Earth Mudra in front of genitals*

Let water be still *belly-*	*Make Water Mudra in front of button*
Let fire be still	*Make Fire Mudra in front of solar plexus*
Let air be still	*Make Air Mudra in front of heart*
Let aether too be still *throat*	*Make Circle Mudra in front of*

For I am a Magician about to utter Sacred Names

The opening line is the Orphic Oath - "I am a child of Earth and Starry Heaven". The following lines derive from early (C2-3) Greek magickal texts, and are useful in that they work up the chakras from Muladhara to Vishuddha, the centre of active magickal power, and of course the voice (the mudras being made to emphasise the element and the links with the appropriate chakras working up the spine).

If you wished to use this to clear the space as well, then you might extend it by visualizing a gold or blue sphere (or other colour of preference) being formed around you as you turn. A standard way to see the sphere being cast is to see flames of the appropriate colour rising up and leaping down to encapsulate you. As you move around see the flames spreading, like segments of an orange, until you are totally surrounded.

4   The 9 Gates & The Magick Sphere

We use the directions to align ourselves, and as a convenient interface for energies. We know air is not only in the east, but it is convenient for group work and discussion to have an agreed structure to work with. If you are doing a ritual by the sea and the waters are in the south, you are not going to invoke water in the west, are you?

Structures are useful but must be flexible and easily adaptable to circumstances. To this end I include a set of attributions for the planets to the directions in the magickal sphere, as worked in a group I was in many years ago, which is consistent with the classical elemental attributions, and works very well when practiced. For planetary workings you might like to try having the altar in the suggested direction given here and see if you notice any changes in the energies and your work.

There are eight gates around the magick circle. The ninth gate, the Gate of the Soul or Self (corresponding to Venus/Love, which can also be represented by the Ankh, symbol of Life), is the point in the centre of the sphere/circle, the axis mundi.

If we look at the eight gates around the circle, they naturally lend themselves to the positions they occupy. Hence the two earthy planets (Saturn, Earth) are in the north and northeast, the two airy ones (Mercury, Jupiter) in the east and southeast, the two fiery ones (Sun, Mars) in the south and southwest, and the two watery ones (Neptune, Moon) in the west and northwest. The four axles of the wheel also imply a natural progression (life to death, quests to answers, etc):

Gate of Acceptance	→	Gate of Ordeals & Expulsions
Gate of Life & Quests	→	Gate of Death & Answers
Gate of Devotion & Contemplation	→	Gate of Shades & Spirits (other realms)
Gate of Knowledge & Power	→	Gate of the Veil of the Mysteries

The remaining planetary attributions, of Uranus to the stars above and Pluto to the underworld below, are both implied by their nature, leaving Venus as the planetary energy for the centre of the circle. This is also appropriate as Venus is love, the most powerful force in the universe.

This system of planetary attributions and the nine gates can easily be incorporated into most contemporary systems, e.g. the Wiccan Wheel of the Year, the Norse Nine Worlds, etc.

The 9 Gates

NE – The Gate of Acceptance

The traditional gate into the circle, between earth and air, is planet Earth, which has the Kala mantra VITRIOL ascribed to it. The attribution of this mantra, with its meaning, of "visit the interior of the earth and there by rectification to find the hidden stone" is clearly apparent. It also illustrates the link between the physical and the spiritual – to find the Philosopher's Stone, the true will or perfect self, one must look within and not discard the physical in the search for perfection.

E – The Gate of Life & Quests

The place of beginnings is the obvious place for Mercury. The quicksilver energy of thought is what produces the questions, the desire to find out and to grow. This process engages us in life's path and reminds us that life is its own reward.

SE – The Gate of Devotion & Contemplation

Jupiter is the religious energy, and so it fits well with the theme of devotion and contemplation. Between air and fire is highly appropriate for Jupiter, which also has a fiery component to its nature.

S – The Gate of Knowledge & Power

As the starfire of our solar system, the Sun is naturally in the place of fire. The solar energy represents the power of light and life, and the knowledge that comes through knowledge of the self (the inner sun).

SW – The Gate of Ordeals & Expulsions

Martial energy often produces strife, and so it is unsurprising that ordeals should be associated with Mars. Between fire and water, Mars is like the steam, a violent reaction between two differing types of energy. Martial energies can be harsh, but are usually necessary and can be very positive for clearing out deadwood. Likewise we do sometimes have to do magick to deal with negativity from people, so expulsions, and the cutting out of your sphere of influence of negative influences and people can be a necessary part of being more efficient with your energy, and hence developing.

W – The Gate of Death & Answers

The west is the place of death in a variety of cultures, from the Egyptian Amenti (underworld) in the west to Britain being seen as the underworld by the Gallo-Germanic tribes, being over the waters in the west from Europe. The trident of Neptune also symbolises one of the most obvious statements you can make, but one that is often forgotten, i.e. that a question may have more than one answer (symbolised by the three prongs of the trident, representing different answers to a question).

NW – The Gate of Shades & Spirits (other realms)

The Moon has long been associated with the dead and the ethereal, so the Moon is well placed here between the energies of water and earth, both of which are influenced by the lunar energies.

N – The Gate of the Veil of the Mysteries

Saturn is the giver of form, and the bearer of the keys of the mysteries of time. As the North is often considered the place of mystery, and the solidity of earth, Saturn finds a natural place here on the circle.

Centre – The Gate of the Soul & Self

For the soul to be free, and the self to grow, you must love yourself. Not the narcissistic self-love of the ego, but the unconditional love of Venus, the Agapé or spiritual love that is unconditional and unrestrictive.

David Rankine

5   Angle Webs

I created this technique in 1987, after considering sigilisation
techniques and playing with ideas for sigilising a moment in
time. Angle Webs are sigils created by superimposing a
macrocosmic / microcosmic map (i.e. the Tree of Life,
representing both the universe and man) onto an astrological
map of a given moment in time.

The sigil acts as a focus for a given moment in space and time,
enabling you to tap into the energy of, e.g. an eclipse, significant
astrological conjunction, nuclear blast, historical event, etc.

How to create an Angle Web:
1. Draw 10 concentric circles at equal intervals outwards from
a central point.

2. Very lightly draw 12 equidistant radii to the outer circle,
dividing all the circles into 12 equal segments. These divisions
represent the astrological signs, so start where you want Aries
to be, and the other signs follow round in an anti-clockwise
direction.

3. The centre of the circle represents the planet Earth (because this is Malkuth qabalistically, and because that is where we are, so that is where we want to focus the energy!). Moving out from the centre the planets are placed on the circumferences of the respective circles relative to their mean distance from Earth, and based on their astrological position at the time the sigil is being drawn for.

In order out from the centre, the planets follow this sequence - Moon, Mars, Venus, Mercury, Sun, Jupiter, Saturn, Uranus, Neptune, Pluto. Thus if the sign of Aries began at the "top" of the page, and the Moon was 28° Taurus, the Moon would be located at approximately the "2 o clock" position on the rim of the first circle.

4. When all the planets have been marked in their respective places on their respective circles, each planet should be joined to the other planets it would be connected to on the Tree of Life, using the standard attributions. Hence the centre, Earth (Malkuth), would be joined to the Moon (Yesod) on the first circle, Venus (Netzach) on the third circle and Mercury (Hod) on the fourth circle.

I am using the classic attribution of Saturn to Binah on the Tree of Life, and Uranus to Daath. Following on from this Neptune is attributed to Chokmah and Pluto to Kether.

5. After all the planets have been connected, the Angle Web is constructed, and ready for empowering by whatever means the operator prefers for use. Obvious modifications to this technique would be using the Qabalistic Colour Scales, body fluids, crystals, etc.

Angle Webs work very well as empowering sigils with a second sigil on top of them, like a Nightside Square, particularly if used in conjunction with their appropriate Mantra Webs. When creating a sigil of particular time, it is up to the operator to decide if they feel the implications of an event would cause problems, e.g. an Angle Web of a nuclear test blast might be preferable to Hiroshima, particularly if you believe in karma.

Angle Web for the First Nuclear Bomb Blast at 12.29.21 p.m. GMT on 16.7.45

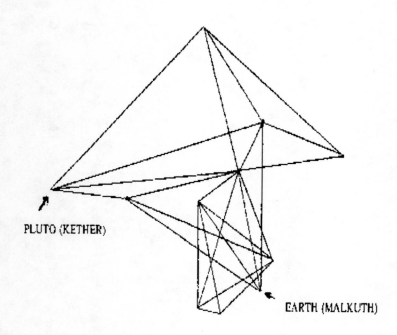

PLUTO (KETHER)

EARTH (MALKUTH)

David Rankine

6   Mantra Webs

The Mantra Web is a very simple technique for using sonics in a group, with a minimum of at least two people. Choose an appropriate mantra with a number of syllables equal to the number of people, e.g. IAO for three people.

The operators should link hands, left palm up and right palm down, and slowly start to circle (clockwise or anti-clockwise according to the nature of the rite) each vibrating their syllable. As this is done, each operator projects a thread of light from their solar plexus (Manipura chakra) to a central focal point (this may be an object or a point in space). The colour(s) of the threads of light should be pre-determined as appropriate to the nature of the rite and parts played by the operators.

As the speed and resonance of the mantra (and circling movement) is built up over a period of time, so the web is empowered, until a climax is reached and the web energy directed by a pre-specified operator with a set signal (gesture or sound, etc) to its purpose.

Using appropriately coloured cords making relevant shapes (triangle, pentagram, circle, etc) will further increase and contain the energy. If the operators vibrate their syllables alternately instead of together, the mantra will *spin* around the circle and have a disorientating effect on the operators that can help alter consciousness dramatically.

Spinning a mantra works better in a confined space, as the rebounding effect of the walls helps enhance and contain the effect. This is not to say that this technique will not work outdoors, of course. Experimentation with this technique will produce a variety of alternatives suitable for different applications.

The Spinning Mantra as given in Liber Al is especially good to use for larger groups, with at least one person vibrating each line of the mantra, in turn. This works best if each person starts their part of the mantra or their syllable as the previous person(s) are just finishing theirs, so there is no break in the sound.

A ka dua
Tu fur biu
Bi aa chefu
Dudu nera
An nuteru

English Translation from the Egyptian
Unity uttermost showed! I adore the might of Thy breath, Supreme and Terrible Deity, Who makes the Gods and even Death to tremble before Thee: I, I adore Thee!

7   Nightside Squares

The Nightside Squares are a series of sigils akin to Abra-Melin Squares (see *The Sacred Magic of Abra-Melin the Mage*). They came about through a series of workings I performed with Grey Fox in 1987-88 at a variety of sacred sites around Britain. Each has different suggested uses for the type of energy they represent, and appropriate Mantra Webs and methods of activation.

Goddess as Cosmic Dancer   K I A

Colours: Gold ($^{K}_{I}A$)   M

            Blue ($_{N}^{I}A$)   N I A

            Black (M)

Mantra: KiaNia

Activate: Inverse Black Pentagram with a Central Red Circle

Power of the Void / In-Between Spaces N I A
Colours: Black   A
Mantra: NiaLia   O
Activate: Gold Line (\) from N to O, Red Line (/) from top
              A to O

Binding & Closing   N I A
Colours: Red   - -
Mantra: LiaNia   A I N
Activate: Central Black Circle with a Red Dot in Centre of
              Circle

Divination   T A O
Colours: Gold   E
Mantra: KiaMia   H R U
Activate: Red Circle quartered with Black X in Centre of
              Square

Power of the Deep Waters   T A L A M
Colours: Black   A   A
Mantra: KiaLiaNia   N   L
Activate: Deep Blue Anti-Clockwise I   A
              Spiral to Centre from M T^h I N A T

8   The Prime Qabalah

I make no apologies for enjoying gematria. I have always enjoyed mathematics and so it was inevitable I was going to enjoy playing with numbers to spark intuitional leaps.

I will qualify my attitude to gematria here by stating that I use it to produce insights or realisations, if a number hasn't prodded some sort of connections within about fifteen seconds, I am not going to spend hours trying to make it, or follow tortuous tunnels of strange number connections.

A few years ago when playing with ideas for numbers, an obvious thought struck me. As English is our spoken language, why not see if a satisfactory system of gematria could be inspired, rather than using Hebrew or Greek Qabalah.

The common systems used for the English alphabet are the uninspiring consecutive A=1 to Z=26 or the same 1 to 26 range with an 11 interval (A=1, L=2, W=3, etc). The latter system, known as English Qabalah and derived from Liber Al, at least makes use of the magickal number eleven (important as the 1 beyond 10, representing the unseen energies) in the attribution of number to letter, but still seems unsatisfactory.

The obvious thought was, why not attribute the 26 prime numbers under 100 (i.e. 10^2) to the letters of the alphabet. Primes are by their nature more magickal, being non-divisible by any other numbers except themselves and one. A further thought was the first 5 primes are under 10, so attribute them to the vowels, and the remaining numbers to the consonants.

The range of numbers attributed to the letters is considerably larger, so there will be higher values attributed to most words, giving a higher degree of significance to correspondences between words attributed to the same number. The attributions suggested are thus:

A	1	H	29	O	5	U	7
B	11	I	3	P	53	V	73
C	13	J	31	Q	59	W	79
D	17	K	37	R	61	X	83
E	2	L	41	S	67	Y	89
F	19	M	43	T	71	Z	97
G	23	N	47				

I include a few of the connections I have noted at this stage for your consideration, doubtless there will be many more as more

time is spent on it. There is an interesting set of connections in the series
119-121 (all magickal numbers: 119 reduces to 11, 120 is 5! and the sum of the series 1-15, 121 is 11^2)
119: Live, Sebek, Son, Time, Veil
120: Death, Magick, Peacock, Soul, Ten
121: Coral, Gemini, Hadit, Law, Love, Sun

As a Thelemite I was amused by Beast, Desire and Sex all adding to 152, and my witchy side found the words altar and woman both adding to 175 entertaining when considering the lines of the Great Rite ("in days of old when woman was the altar ..."), and also Wheel and Year both adding to 153. Angel and Demon both adding to 114 is another good one! Many pairs of words equate which provoke thought, e.g. for 115 we have both Chaos and Change, and at 211 both Mother and Daughter.

Applying the Prime Qabalah (PQ) to Liber Al produces some stunning results and gives a new view of some of the ciphers and keys in this text. To illustrate, Al 1.24 "I am Nuit, and my word is six and fifty." Starting with the obvious consideration, what word adds to 56 in PQ? I decided on preferably a 2-letter word as implied by the term "six and fifty" rather than saying "fifty-six". The one which jumped to mind was Pi (P = 53 + I = 3). And how perfect is this as the word of Nuit!

The relationship between the radius of a circle with its circumference and area fits extremely well with the concept of Nuit as the eternal circle, linked by the straight line (the radius) to the point in the centre that is Hadit. Also Pi is an irrational number, being indefinable, which is totally appropriate for the Goddess Who represents infinite space.

Al 1.40 reads "Who calls us Thelemites will do no wrong, if he look but close into the word. For there are therein Three Grades, the Hermit, and the Lover, and the Man of Earth. Do what thou wilt shall be the whole of the Law." We all know Thelema means Will in English. In PQ Will adds to 164, as do Holy, Heart and Earth.

These three words easily lend themselves to the three grades described, and also to the subtle body by the implications of the words.

Holy – Hermit – Crown chakra
Heart – Lover – Heart chakra
Earth – Man of Earth – Base chakra

This also then implies that the three grades are not consecutive, but rather represent the emphasis of where you choose to focus your energies at a given moment in your life.

II.15 reads "For I am perfect, being Not; and my number is nine by the fools; but with the just I am eight, and one in eight: Which is vital, for I am none indeed. The Empress and the King are not of me; for there is a further secret." By PQ Not adds to 133, the same as Circle and Diamond. The Circle is the perfect form which Nuit describes Herself as, and Diamond is the most perfect stone.

Looking at the numbers, 8 is the combination of I and 0, and 1 in 8 is A added in the middle i.e. the IAO formula. So I am none indeed see the New Analysis of IAO (Chapter 11).

9   Beyond the Numerical Horizon – Inspirational Gematria

Gematria is one of those subjects that often tend to be ignored, or cause people to glaze over. However it is an extremely useful magickal tool. Having created the Prime Qabalah, I decided to explore and expound the field with respect to the English alphabet and language.

With classic Hebrew gematria, the usual methods are standard gematria, i.e. adding up the numerical values of the letters and comparing them to other words of the same total, Notariqon, which is essentially creating an acronym from the first letters of the words in a sentence, and Temurah, which is a replacement of letters by juxtaposing letters with other letters on a set scale of change.

As I am working with English, I decided to use English terms for the techniques. Apart from standard gematria, there are six other techniques I feel relevant and worth considering for magickal use.

Contraction

Notariqon by another name. A very good technique for creating power or barbarous words. In the past this technique has been used to produce divine names and magickal formulae, e.g. AGLA, ARARITA, INRI, VITRIOL, etc.

Equation

Standard gematria. Looking at the numerical value of a word and comparing other words of the same value. This is then used to produce intuitional leaps and possibly shift consciousness through the mind's response to the connections made between symbols and concepts. Examples of this would be the PQ for 114 being both angel & demon, and 115 being both chaos & change.

Expansion

A useful technique for exploring the unconscious and discovering its contents. As the name suggests, it is essentially the opposite of contraction. Rather than reducing a sentence to a word, you allow the mind to produce a sentence from a word. This can be used as a form of automatic writing, allowing the mind to empty whatever springs up, until it is exhausted. This also allows for consciousness shifts which may then be used for whatever desired purpose. E.g. considering the word IAO, the mind might produce phrases like I Adore Orgasms, or In Ancient Oracles, etc.

Reversal

A technique best exemplified by Charles Stansfield Jones (Frater Achad) and his reversal of the divine name AL to produce LA, and hence reveal one of the keys of Liber Al (*The Book of the Law*). Another good technique for stimulating the mind through revealing alternative meanings and reversing the natural order. Classic examples are such words as God/Dog (Al II.19) and Live/Evil.

Sliding

Temurah expanded. An interesting way to produce numbers for comparison and barbarous words relevant to the nature of the magickal operation. By applying a "slide" of a number appropriate to the operation, words become a bizarre mixture of barbarous, nonsensical terms. So for a Jupiterian ritual, you might shift all the letters along 4 places, with A becoming E, B becoming F, etc.

Transfiguration

Looking within a word to find other words or phrases, to allow intuitional leaps and realisations. E.g. the word "manifestation" contains the words "Maat infest ions", which might be interpreted as Maat permeates charged particles, providing an interesting slant to Liber Al I.1, and also emphasising the relationship between Nuit and Maat.

Transposition

Essentially anagrams. Making a word into another word by rearranging all the letters, and seeing what inspiration it provides. So e.g. Rose/Eros, Mars/Rams, Team/Mate, etc.

As can be seen from these techniques, there is a wide range of ways we can use words and number for magickal work and shifting our consciousness. It is time for English gematria to come of age and assume its place as one of the easiest tools for anyone to use, even people with a phobia of number!

David Rankine

10   The Esoteric Symbolism
of the Hebrew
Alphabet

The Hebrew alphabet contains many mysteries in itself. This chapter is an attempt to demonstrate some of the qualities of the letters not commonly discussed. These ideas are put across as concepts to play with and meditate on for insight, not as absolutes. They are also a reminder that we should not take things for granted in magick, and always explore to the limits and beyond.

Aleph

Represents the first swirlings, the primal energy in motion. The swastika as a symbol of energy in motion is another form of aleph. When we look at a picture of a hurricane or tornado building up, we can see why air in its energising aspect is attributed to aleph. Note also that Aleph indicates the formula of pranayama - the air in the breath (Aleph) is focused (Lamed) and directed through the mouth (Pe). Aleph is the first of the three mother letters, and can also be seen as the Great Mother becoming aware and beginning to manifest i.e. create/give birth to form.

Beth

On a microcosmic level Beth represents the womb, on a macrocosmic level it is the pregnant void, full of potential and unmanifest energy (which later manifests as the Tau which is the final letter of Beth (BITh). Beth can also be considered to symbolise the unconscious as the storehouse of potential and experience. In alchemy Beth could be considered both the crucible and the spirit bottle in which transformation takes place. The central Yod in Beth also indicates the symbolism of fertilization and the balance of opposites creating a greater whole – the womb (Beth) is fertilized by the sperm (Yod) giving balance and realisation of potential (Tau).

Gimel

Is the letter of initiation. As the camel stores water in its hump to endure the desert conditions, so Gimel contains Mem, the letter whose meaning is water. Mem also symbolises orgasm, the Kalas and the Great Mother, so this also indicates the autosexual formula of devotion, offering your energies to the Great Goddess to align yourself with Her flow, a necessary step in the process of initiation. For what is initiation but a personal transformation induced by alignment to a particular current of energy? That Gimel ends with the letter Lamed directs the attention to the focus that the magician must achieve to maintain his/her will. Without focus one will wander like a stray in the desert, but Gimel offers the promise that alignment with the correct energies encourages initiation, enabling one to find the path and survive the rigours of the desert journey.

Daleth

Represents the yoni (especially the labia), and corresponds to such appropriate symbols as the cauldron and the chalice. Also it is the gateway, leading to the womb/pregnant void (again the final Tau in Daleth [DLTh] indicating the manifestation from the unmanifest void). The focus indicated by the central Lamed in Daleth also suggests the formula of female arousal to generate oracular states, the accessing of the unmanifest potential of creation indicated by the womb and the feminine.

He

The twin pillars of the Tree, in this context symbolising the legs, emphasised by the repeat spelling i.e. two of the same thing. In the same context He could also symbolise the Ida and Pingala energy channels in the subtle body. By its meaning of window, He indicates air. As a feminine letter which is a twin spelling, He could also symbolise the formula of the twin light/dark Goddess, as depicted by deities such as Isis and Nephthys.

Vau

The twin spelling of vau indicates the twin states of the phallus (flaccid and erect). Can also be seen as the wand, the double quality recalling the caduceus. That He and Vau, which correspond to the numbers 5 and 6, are the only two letters spelt by repetition of themselves is highly significant – these numbers symbolise the pentagram and hexagram, man and the universe, and can be seen as an expression of the whole in the formula of "As above, so below". This is reinforced by the addition of the two numbers spelt in full to produce 22 (10 for HH + 12 for VV, the only two letters spelt in full by repetition of themselves), the total number of letters in the Hebrew alphabet and hence indicative of the whole. As He represents the twin Goddess, so the masculine Vau can also be seen as the twin God of order/chaos, such as Osiris and Set.

Zain

Means sword, and symbolises those qualities associated with

the sword like will, intuition, and discrimination. Also represents the lightning flash of creative energy (aka the flaming sword). The letters which comprise Zain also indicate the formula of personal growth through change and dealing with baggage – the sword (Zain) wielded by the hand (Yod) brings transformation through necessary death (Nun).

Cheth

Means fence, and indicates the boundaries between the seen and the unseen. The combination of the fence (Cheth), or yoni, and the sperm (Yod), giving form to the unmanifest potential (Tau), and demonstrating the sexual aspect of the Great Work which Cheth represents. If the Yod is seen as the hand, this letter can also represent the power of Woman as oracle, without the need for male energy, as the yoni (Cheth) is stimulated by the hand (Yod) to give access to visions of the future i.e. unmanifest potential (Tau).

Teth

The dual symbolism of the serpent as male and female is seen in the spelling of Teth; the male is represented by the Yod indicating the sperm, and the female by the final Tau indicating the wisdom and transformative powers of the serpent. The initial teth itself can be seen as indicating the kundalini.

Yod

Represents the hand as the giver of form, the activity which occurs as manifestation at the end of the process of realisation. Also represents the sperm, as the point of manifestation. If we look at its spelling, we also see the symbolism of Yod as representing lovemaking rather than simply sex, combining the hand and activity (Yod), the phallus (Vau) and the labia and yoni (Daleth).

Kaph
Is another dualistic letter in its symbolism. The palm (kaph) can indicate receptivity, by its emptiness, or action by its readiness to move. This is further emphasised by the final Pe, as the mouth can receive (food and drink) or act (by talking, kissing etc).

Lamed
In many ways perhaps the strangest letter in the Hebrew alphabet, Lamed (ox-goad) represents the focus of energies to achieve intent. Lamed also reminds us of a lesson that men often find difficult, namely that the focus (Lamed) achieved through either sexual union or the Great Mother (Mem) is ultimately from a feminine source (Daleth). Thus the ox-goad is used to control the ox (masculine energies), and submission to the will of the Goddess is a necessary step on the path to fulfillment – which needs to be learned to overcome the masculine desire for control.

Mem
Represents the formula of sexual union – orgasm and the production of the Kalas. The sperm (Yod) is surrounded by the sexual fluids (waters) of Mem, producing the Kalas. Mem, a mother letter, also symbolises the Great Mother, Who gives birth to the universe and from Whose yoni flows the Kalas which comprise existence.

Nun
Represents the primal waters from which life sprang. On the microcosmic level it represents the menstrual blood, and the elixir rubae (mixed sexual fluids and blood) used in sex magick; the two Nun's symbolising menstrual blood have the phallus of Vau inserted between them. In alchemical terms

Nun symbolises generation from putrefaction, birth from the base materials, as with the symbolism of the lotus growing from the mud.

Samekh

With its meaning of support and shape, Samekh can be seen as symbolising the serpent ouroboros, surrounding the world in a circle. The first letter (Samekh) indicates the propping or supporting of ideas, i.e. the perseverance and resolution to "uphold" a belief or a course of action. For this reason truth as the natural order of things is also symbolised by this letter. The central Mem also indicates the implied union or combination of opposites implied by a support, keeping two things in harmony. The dualistic theme is maintained through the final Kaph, indicating both receptivity and action, each as required, i.e. when needed to support right action and thinking.

Ayin

As meaning eye represents vision (both normal and spirit through the third eye) and the yoni as the eye to the womb and potential. Sexual union and the production of the Kalas is also indicated by the composition of Ayin – the yoni (Ayin) is the crucible for the sperm (Yod) and the menstrual blood (Nun) to mingle and form the alchemical union of the opposites that they represent. The vision and change of perspective provided by the sexual union opens the eyes to really see, i.e. know your will.

Pe

Represents the magick of the mouth – the logos, speech and hence the oracle. The oracle is particularly indicated by the combination of the letters when spelt in full – Pe (mouth) and He (divination). On a sexual level the final He can be interpreted as the legs, so the formula of oral sex is then implied by the tongue "between" the legs, as it were.

Tzaddi

Is the gateway of the boundaries between realms. As the fish-hook (Tzaddi) brings the fish from the water (unconscious) onto the land (conscious) where it can be eaten, so it enables the body to be maintained and the will enacted through activity. Tzaddi represents the process of establishing the link between the conscious and unconscious mind so the power of the mind can be accessed at will. To this end the presence of the gateway (Daleth) and activity (Yod) to draw out the information (Tzaddi) required for realisation. The sexual nature of Daleth and Yod as representing the yoni and sperm or hand are also worth noting as methods of helping this process of realisation occur.

Qoph

Curiously means "back of the head", until we consider that it corresponds to the pineal gland on the microcosmic level; on a macrocosmic level it corresponds to the moon - the satellite which reflects and influences through the tides - hence it also corresponds to sorcery and the left hand path (in the sense of the vama marg of tantra, using unusual/taboo methods to achieve gnosis) which emphasise the Dionysian liberation/ecstasy rather than the Apollonian illumination. Looking at the composition of Qoph, it is comprised of Qoph (back of the head) and Pe (mouth), which also indicates the formula of oracular work, receiving inspiration and manifesting it through speech.

Resh

Microcosmically it represents the centre of consciousness, the head as the repository of the soul; macrocosmically it is the Sun, the star as the centre of a universe. Not just the Sun or star, but also the starfire, the radiance from the star and its effects, as seen by the Yod (activity) and Shin (fire) that comprise the rest of the letter. The central Yod could also indicate the autosexual formula as generating personal sexual fire/energy. Resh can also indicate divine wisdom, as in the case of the severed head oracle (e.g. Bran, Mimir, Orpheus, etc), and as illumination (the solar, Apollonian path).

Shin

Is the third and final mother letter, and as such represents the Triple Goddess, indicated by the three "tongues" of the letter. Spelt in full (ShIN) it adds to 360, indicating the circle (as the number of degrees) which is another Goddess glyph. Considering the letters which comprise Shin, we can see the sperm (Yod) and menstrual blood (Nun) infused with the energy of spirit to produce the elixir vitae, the sexual expression of the Philosopher's Stone.

Tau

Represents the equal armed cross of balance, the combination of elements. Also represents the material plane of existence, the universe (the final Vau indicating the hexagram symbolising the universe). As the final letter of the alphabet, Tau also symbolises the void from which the first swirlings of creation (Aleph) sprang. Combined these first and last letters make ATh – the Essence, i.e. the manifestation into matter (Tau) from the unmanifest potential which starts to awaken with the first swirlings (Aleph).

11 A New Analysis of IAO

I have long felt that the IAO formula is one of the most powerful in magick, and the standard attribution of the slain god formula of Osiris through the Isis, Apophis, Osiris combination only scratches the surface of possible uses for this formula. When vibrating the IAO formula during a ritual in 1992 the phrase "I am One, I am None" came into my head, expressed in the form below as a visual image containing IAO.

I	I
Am	Am
One	nOne

Subsequent examination of the combination of letters which comprise this word sigil produced very interesting results, giving a list of eleven "deity" words that can easily be linked to the eleven planetary energies and 11 other significant words which all link in to the formula. This formula can hence be seen as a combination of all the planetary energies, and be used very effectively for planetary ritual, as a mantra (I am One, I am None), or in its written form as a sigil to focus energy, either

by itself or incorporated into a more complex sigil or a
mandala.

The nOne, or 0 = 1 formula is perhaps the central essence of
this magickal formula i.e. the removal of subject and object
(absence of personal identity and transcendence of Maya or
illusion) in the universal web of being (the Tao/Wyrd/etc). This
is emphasised by the occurrence of the contraindicating 0
forms (Ain/Anon/Nemo/Nema – which all refer to nothingness
or absence of identity) and the 1 forms (Ani/Man/Name/Nia
– which all link to identity and gender). The remaining forms
give the basis of ritual - force (Ia), form (omen) and place
(nome).

The 11 Deities

1.   Aion, Mithraic Time God, who symbolises Saturn (as
     time).
2.   Amen or Amun, Egyptian Fertility God, who is Solar
     in nature.
3.   An or Anu, Sumerian Deity of Heaven, Jupiterian in
     nature and by His role in the pantheon.
4.   Ao, the four Chinese Dragon Kings, Deities of Rain &
     Sea and so symbolising Earth as the terrestrial waters.
5.   Ea, or as He is also known, Enki, Sumerian God of
     Magick and the Tides, Who is Neptunian in His nature.
6.   Ennoia, the Gnostic Personification of Thought,
     representing Mercury.
7.   Io, the Maori God of Eternity, corresponds to the
     Plutonian energy through the Qabalistic idea of Pluto
     as Kether, the eternal Godhead.
8.   Maie or Maia, the Indian Goddess of Illusion, which is
     Lunar in nature
9.   Min, the Egyptian God of Sex, a Venusian energy.

10. Nemain, the Celtic War Goddess Whose name means Frenzy, is obviously Martial.

11. Om, the Sanskrit mantra that represents the Sound of the Universe, and I consider Uranian as the starry heavens that comprise the universe.

The 11 Other Words

1. Ain = Void (Hebrew) – nothingness (a 0 form).
2. Ani = I, Myself (Hebrew) – the personal identity (a 1 form).
3. Anon = Unknown – an unidentified individual through choice (a 0 form).
4. Ia = Primal Word of Magick (cf OM), the sound which represents the energy or force put into a magickal act, creative energy as the logos.
5. Iam = Already, Now (Latin) = Time.
6. Man = Male – the masculine energy (a 1 form).
7. Name = Defining Quality – the expression of identity (a 1 form).
8. Nemo/a = Nobody (Latin m/f forms) – absence of ego or personal identity (a 0 form).
9. Nia = Daughter (Hebrew) = Female – the feminine energy (a 1 form).
10. Nome = Sacred Place (Egyptian) – a place where deity is more present, so in this case it represents the place the magick is worked in as the point of action or manifestation.
11. Omen = Sign – a physical manifestation of energy symbolising an action or event, so literally an omen is the form taken to represent the force.

This analysis is included to demonstrate the way that analysis can reveal layers of symbolism and use in a phrase. Such analysis is especially worth applying to barbarous words if they turn up in your magickal work.

By barbarous words I mean strange combinations of sounds which may sound like nonsense in any language you are aware of, but which ring with a resonance of power due to the combination of sounds. If you do find such words come to you, write them down as they sound to you and keep them for further study after your magick. You may also find such words come to you in dreams, or through people who are in deep trance acting as an oracle.

12   The Kalas

I first came across the concept of the Kalas in Kenneth Grant's writings. So I wanted to know, what are the Kalas? The word Kala means cycle of time or energy, and is derived from Kali, the Universal Goddess who both Creates and destroys the Universe. Kalas can also mean "rays" or "emanations", indicating that on a symbolic level the Kalas can be seen as the flows of energy from the yoni of Kali as She gives birth to the universe. You should note that the perception of the Kalas I am describing here as a working system is quite different to that described in Kenneth Grant's works.

On a macrocosmic level the Kalas represent the energy flows which make up everything. On a microcosmic level the Kalas are the charged sexual fluids empowered through sex magick. In the system I created there are sixteen Kalas, which correspond to the classic five Elements and eleven Astrological Planets traditionally used in magick. I have since discovered that this is borne out in some of the Tantras, which also work with sixteen Kalas.

However it should be stated that one of the main formulae, that of consumption of the charged sexual fluids, requires a book all of its own, and brings into consideration other neglected considerations like the 12-petalled Kala chakra at the base of the tongue. I will not cover this particular aspect of working with the Kalas in this volume.

The Vishuddha chakra as Centre of Active Magickal Power is especially relevant to practitioners of this system. This chakra is also the Centre of Dreaming, and its 16 petals correspond to the Kalas. That the sixteenth Kala should correspond to Spirit, also verifying the attributions of the other four elements and planetary energies as the basis of all energies is demonstrated in the tantric text, the Lalitashasranama, where we find the following quotes.

"The 16th Kala is the Nectar of Supreme Excellence"

"The Moon shows 15 phases in Her waxing and waning. The 16th part, when Time stands still, is when and where Divinity incarnates."

Magickal techniques may require the use of more than one Kala, which may be achieved by combining the symbols, tools, scents, etc of the required Kalas. This system of attributions is compatible with pretty much any system of magick you may choose to work, and makes a simple structure to work with. As I have already observed, magick works best when it is kept simple and not over-complicated with unnecessary complexities. Raising energy, exaltation of consciousness and directed will (i.e. intent) are the prime requisites of magickal action.

It is inevitable that there will be a degree of overlap between Kalas, as there is between chakras, and the operator(s) should decide which Kala is most appropriate to use for an operation. This list is not exhaustive, and should be used for reference rather than as an absolute.

The Space Kala

CORRESPONDS: Pluto

MAGICKS   Invisibility, Location Magicks (inc.
                Treasure Finding) Stellar Magicks

SYMBOL   Crown

COLOUR   White

SCENTS   Almond, Amaranth

CRYSTALS   Diamond, Fluorite

TOOLS   Helmet, Hood, Keys, Lamp

HERBS   Fly Agaric, Psilocybin Mushrooms

MATERIALS   Ebony, Platinum

ANIMALS   Crane, Crayfish, Dog, Swan, Wolf,
                Dragons

PLANTS   Almond, Amaranth, Cypress, Fungi

SIGIL

The Space Kala is one to use to tap potential - the potential of
the vastness of space. Hence it is also associated with the
practice of astral projection and its ultimate form, bilocation.

Due to the classical attribution of Pluto, symbolising treasure and the wealth found in the earth (the metals, gems, etc), this Kala is also associated with locating treasure and lost objects. This Kala could be used in magicks to aid in locating "lost" people as well, like friends one has lost touch with, or distant (or close) family. When magicks have misfired and you need to restore or regenerate the web of energies around you, use this Kala.

The Tidal Kala

CORRESPONDS:	Neptune
MAGICKS	Mercanthropy, Sea Lore, Tidal Magicks
SYMBOL	Trident
COLOUR	Grey
SCENTS	Musk
CRYSTALS	Bezoar, Crabs Eye, Pearl, Rutile Quartz
TOOLS	Conch, Net
HERBS	Mescalin, Peyote
MATERIALS	Shell, Tungsten
ANIMALS	Albatross, Dolphin, Fish, Heron, Horse, Octopus, Sea Horse, Sea-Urchin, Shark, Whale, Capricorn Goat, Kelpi, Kraken, Meliai, Mer-Creatures, Sea Serpents, Sirens
PLANTS	Anemone, Ash, Dulse & other Sea Weeds, Orchid, Plankton

SIGIL

Tides and currents affect many things, not just the sea. Likewise the Tidal Kala can be used for works other than those connected with the sea. The tides of menstruation, and emotional cycles like depression, may also benefit from using this Kala as a prophylactic. If for any reason you are planning on using psychotropic substances for magickal work, use this Kala to help you ride the effects and not be controlled by them. The Tidal Kala is appropriate for those times when you feel "out of sync", or that you are going against the flow of events and things are going badly in your life. The Tidal Kala is also of course good for any magicks connected with the sea and her denizens.

The Time Kala

CORRESPONDS: Saturn

MAGICKS Equilibrium (inc. legal matters), Restrictive Magicks, Time Magicks

SYMBOL Sickle & Scythe

COLOUR Black

SCENTS Asafoetida, Civet, Myrrh, Sulphur

CRYSTALS Jet, Obsidian, Smoky Quartz

TOOLS Scales, Shadows, Veil

HERBS Aconite, Belladonna, Datura, Hellebore, Hemlock, Henbane

MATERIALS Lead

ANIMALS Ass, Cow, Crocodile, Crow, Donkey, Goat, Hippopotamus, Amphisbaena, Corpse Candles, Ghouls, Larvae

PLANTS Apple, Cypress, Elm, Holly, Moss, Yew

SIGIL

The Time Kala is very good for restrictive magicks, such as bindings when used in conjunction with other Kalas; with the Web Kala, in the use of cord magick, through such forms as ligature (knots to bind), and the Will Kala through the use of sigils. As the Time Kala is associated with equilibrium, it is very good to use for magickal work concerning justice and legal matters.

This Kala can also work well for astral projection in animal form rather than human. Try the barbarous phrase Ia-Umm Ut-Za as a trigger and shift into an animal of your preference in your astral form. You may find this easier if you visualize a silver pentagram on a black background as an astral doorway and project through the centre of the pentagram, uttering the phrase and shifting as you do.

Also recommended for exploration of time, and reality tunnels through careful work with the other Kalas in the D of Force and Form (i.e. Space and Tidal).

The Devotion Kala

CORRESPONDS:	Jupiter
MAGICKS	Ascendancy, Body Health, Devotion
SYMBOL	Sceptre
COLOUR	Deep Blue
SCENTS	Cedar, Copal, Lavender, Saffron
CRYSTALS	Lapis Lazuli, Sapphire, Sodalite, Turquoise
TOOLS	Crook, Dorje, Mace
HERBS	Valerian, Wild Lettuce
MATERIALS	Tin
ANIMALS	Cuckoo, Goose, Praying Mantis, Ram, Raven, Sturgeon, Wren, Centaur, Gryphon
PLANTS	Agrimony, Alfalfa, Alkanet, Arnica, Bayberry, Betony, Borage, Cedar, Chervil, Cinquefoil, Dock, Fir, Fumitory, Hyssop, Maple, Melissa, Poplar, Sage, Shamrock, Vervain

SIGIL

The Devotion Kala is strongly linked to the mystical energies, i.e. states of gnosis and bliss. This Kala is good to work with during preparation for devotional work, like meditation and fasting. Due to Jupiter's expansive nature it is also a good one to work with to gain the upper hand in a situation, so use it if you are in a tough competition for a job or house, for example. The Devotion Kala can also promote insight during meditation and contemplation, opening the channels in the consciousness wider for greater insights.

This Kala is also a primary Kala in the sense that it may be used (in conjunction with "mundane" methods like good diet and exercise) to promote good bodily health. For some reason many people who practice magick neglect their health, which is bizarre as a good material base (body and environment) are prime requisites for strong and successful magicks.

David Rankine

The Energy Kala

CORRESPONDS: Mars

MAGICKS   Atavistic, Lycanthropy, Strength, Vengeance

SYMBOL   Spear

COLOUR   Scarlet

SCENTS   Capsicum, Dragons Blood, Opoponax, Pepper

CRYSTALS   Bloodstone, Garnet, Jasper, Haematite, Pyrite, Ruby

TOOLS   Anvil, Burin, Hammer, Scourge, Whip

HERBS   Caffeine, Iboga, Tobacco

MATERIALS   Blood, Iron, Lodestone, Magnet

ANIMALS   Bear, Boar, Cock, Horse, Ram, Wolf, Woodpecker, Basilisk, Chimaera, Furies, Hippogrif, Were-Animals

PLANTS   Basil, Bay, Buttercup, Chilli, Hickory, Mustard, Nettle, Pepper, Rue, Thistle

SIGIL

The Energy Kala is also known, in combination with the Will Kala, as *Red Gold*. The combination of these two Kalas gives one of the formulae of the incoming Aeon, that of Horus. Combined, I feel these two Kalas produces one of the most powerful empowering alchemical elixirs possible.

In this day and age the use of blood in ritual is an area that has to be handled with extreme care. For personal work it is not such an issue, but if working with others the highest standards of hygiene should be observed.

Although blood does not have to be used for atavistic work, it increases the magnitude of the changes and power of the work greatly. Blood used in magick stirs the lower levels of the unconscious, and brings up power from the reptilian and simian levels of the brain, which helps the shapeshifting (either astral, emotional or physical) that is desired.

For strength and endurance this Kala is also good to work with, so use the Energy Kala if you are training and building up stamina. It also works well with the Time Kala for works of vengeance if you are righting a serious wrong.

David Rankine

The Will Kala

CORRESPONDS: Sol

MAGICKS   Personal Power, Talismans, Wealth Magicks

SYMBOL   Sword

COLOUR   Gold

SCENTS   Acacia, Cinnamon, Heliotrope, Orange

CRYSTALS   Cats Eye, Hawks Eye, Sunstone, Tigers Eye, Topaz

TOOLS   Cymbals, Lamen, Lance, Rose Cross

HERBS   Calamus, Eyebright, Foxglove, Galangal, Wine

MATERIALS   Gold

ANIMALS   Bee, Falcon, Hawk, Leopard, Lion, Panther, Pelican, Sparrowhawk, Tiger, Phoenix

PLANTS   Angelica, Chamomile, Ginger, Gorse, Jalap, Juniper, Laurel, Marigold, Mistletoe, Oak, Orris, Palm, Pine, Reed, St Johns Wort, Sunflower, Vine

SIGIL

The Will Kala is ideal for talismanic magick, and demonstrates the strength of your will to manifest the desired effect. Sigils being a pictographic representation of intent, they may be enhanced by being drawn and/or with this Kala.

As the will is your primary magickal drive, the importance of strengthening it cannot be overstated. Hence this Kala is a good one to work with regularly to exercise and develop the "muscles" of your will to make it as powerful and efficient as possible. From development of personal power comes improvement in the qualities required for leadership like confidence and decisiveness.

A successful magician should also be able to ensure they have enough to practice their magick in a degree of comfort, so do not be reluctant about using this Kala for wealth magicks to enhance your financial situation. Money is a form of energy, and its manipulation to benefit you is an often ignored skill in magickal circles.

The all-round magician's energy, the Will Kala may be used to strengthen another Kala or in conjunction with the Love Kala when you are not quite sure which to use.

The Love Kala

CORRESPONDS: Venus

MAGICKS — Aphrodisiacs, Emotional Magicks, Fertility Magicks, Self-Confidence

SYMBOL — Belt & Girdle

COLOUR — Emerald

SCENTS — Benzoin, Bergamot, Lilac, Rose, Saunderswood

CRYSTALS — Emerald, Fluorspar, Malachite, Rhodochrosite, Rose Quartz, Zoisite

TOOLS — Harp, Necklace

HERBS — Damiana, Passion Flower, Saw Palmetto

MATERIALS — Copper

ANIMALS — Birds, Dove, Lynx, Nightingale, Partridge, Peacock, Quince, Sow, Sparrow, Incubi, Succubi

PLANTS — Adam & Eve Root, Balm, Clover, Daffodil, Elder, Lady's Mantle, Myrtle, Primrose, Rose, Sycamore, Venus Fly Trap, Violet

SIGIL

The Love Kala is the ideal combination Kala. It may be worked with any other Kala to good effect. Works to improve the emotional state or deal with emotional traumas should be performed with this Kala. To the same end improving self-confidence should be worked on if an issue, as your magick is only as strong as your will.

If your self-confidence is low, so will your willpower be. Magicks to enhance fertility, for human, animal or crop may all also benefit from the use of this Kala. The Love Kala is also useful for times of dryness, when you need to promote ideas and growth, to increase action in your life, hence it is good for "dark nights of the soul".

The Knowledge Kala

CORRESPONDS:	Mercury
MAGICKS	Communication, Healing, Insight, Protection, Science
SYMBOL	Caduceus
COLOUR	Light Blue
SCENTS	Lime, Mace, Mastic, Sandalwood, Storax, Tragacanth
CRYSTALS	Agate, Citrine Quartz, Opal
TOOLS	Apron, Caduceus
HERBS	Absinthe, Hashish, Nutmeg
MATERIALS	Mercury
ANIMALS	Ape, Baboon, Bat, Coyote, Dog, Hermaphrodite, Hummingbird, Kingfisher, Jay, Magpie, Parrot, Salmon, Swallow, Twin Serpents
PLANTS	Dill, Herb Mercury, Liquorice, Marjoram, Moly

SIGIL

The Knowledge Kala can enhance traditional Mercurial magicks, such as healing and protection. It can also be used to enhance powers of communication, develop insights and confidence, as well as discrimination. Works of a scientific nature such as research or merging magick with technology may also be enhanced with this Kala.

I have found use of the Knowledge Kala tends to induce a "Knowledge Trance" state which benefits greatly from having a second person to scribe details of the information that arises in the conscious mind (if working solo, it is worth having a tape recorder set on record with an omni-directional microphone). My experience of the induced trance states has been an average duration of 30 minutes to an hour.

For detailed information, it is worth having your question(s) well prepared, with the precision you would apply to achieving a desired effect using results magick - the more precise you are, the more focused the information you glean tends to be.

The Sorcery Kala

CORRESPONDS: Luna

MAGICKS Astral Work, Clairvoyance,
Communication with Dead,
Dreamwork, Illusions, Poisons,
Sigilisation

SYMBOL Mirror

COLOUR Silver

SCENTS Camphor, Honeysuckle, Jasmine,
Lignum Aloes

CRYSTALS Moonstone, Pearl, Quartz

TOOLS Broom, Bow & Arrow, Perfumes,
Sandals

HERBS Alstonia, Ginseng, Lobelia,
Mandrake, Mugwort, Opium,
Yohimbe

MATERIALS Ivory, Silver

ANIMALS Badger, Cat, Deer, Dog, Elephant,
Frog, Hare, Hyena, Lizards, Rat,
Snail, Stork, Toad, Tortoise,
Ghosts, Lemures, Loons,
Phantoms, Unicorns, Werewolves,
Zombies

PLANTS   Adders Tongue, Alder, Artemisia,
            Hazel, Jojoba, Mangrove,
            Moonwort, Ranunculus,
            Thyme, Tumeric, Willow,
            Witchazel

SIGIL

The Sorcery Kala is also known in one form as White Gold.
The use of this Kala greatly enhances all astral works, including
development of the passive psychic faculties such as
clairvoyance and clairaudience.

The form of the Sorcery Kala produced in this phase is better
for use for techniques such as Communication with the Dead,
Illusions and Poisons. The Red Sorcery Kala can be enhanced
in potency by being produced (when possible) in the dark of
the Moon, and when the Moon is in Scorpio (or ideally both).

Astral work, such as astral projection and remote viewing
(clairvoyance) may benefit from the use of this Kala. Illusions
and mirror work, and lucid dream work can all also be
enhanced with this Kala.

The Nature Kala

CORRESPONDS:	Terra
MAGICKS	Alchemy, Animal Lore, Herb & Plant Lore, Weather Magicks
SYMBOL	Drum
COLOUR	Amber
SCENTS	Dittany of Crete, Vetivert
CRYSTALS	Amber, Aventurine, Crysocolla, Jade, Peridot, Snakestone
TOOLS	Cauldron, Pyramid, Shield
HERBS	Beer, Kava Kava
MATERIALS	Coal, Horn
ANIMALS	Ant, Eagle, Rhinocerus, Serpent, Stag, Dragons, Gorgons, Sphinx, Vampires, Will o' the Wisp
PLANTS	Bamboo, Corn, Hops, Ivy, Lily, Rice, Rowan, Snowdrop, Wheat

SIGIL

The Nature Kala is the Kala of our biosphere. Magicks relating to all that live on the earth may be worked with this Kala, such as animal, herb and plant lore. Likewise magicks to affect the weather and bring or disperse rain, winds etc, may also be performed with this Kala. Alchemical workings, especially with metals or crystals, may also be enhanced with this Kala.

Magicks to bring an ethereal being into physical form (i.e. evocation) may also benefit from working with this Kala. Using a drum (the world shield) placed on the lap when seated for sustained periods of time with monotonous rhythms is a good way to attune to the energies of this Kala, as well as making you feel very horny if male!

The Web Kala

CORRESPONDS :	Uranus
MAGICKS	Reality Magicks
SYMBOL	Web
COLOUR	Purple
SCENTS	Ambergris, Garlic
CRYSTALS	Amethyst, Crysolith, Rhodolite, Sphene, Tourmaline
TOOLS	Bell, Cloak, Cords
HERBS	Harmaline, Morning Glory
MATERIALS	Titanium
ANIMALS	Bee, Butterfly, Camel, Fox, Ibis, Jackal, Jaguar, Moth, Khephra, Spider, Vulture, Wolf
PLANTS	Garlic, Orchid

SIGIL

The Web Kala is the most tricky and in some ways dangerous of the Kalas. It is the Kala that embodies magick, and the interconnectedness of all things. This Kala is best used in works of subtlety, or to attempt to shift the energies in your environment to alter the reality you are in. To this end it may be used for evocation, astral projection and on a bigger scale, to try and shift the reality tunnel you are in at a given moment in time.

Be extremely careful when working with this Kala that your intent is focused and pure, or you may find events going out of your control. Eclipses are a very good time to try and work with this Kala.

The Cyclic Kala

CORRESPONDS : Water

MAGICKS Dissolution, Enchantment, Hydromancy, Purification, Skrying

SYMBOL Cup

COLOUR Blue

SCENTS Benzoin, Karaya, Lotus, Onycha, Ylang Ylang

CRYSTALS Aquamarine, Azurite, Beryl, Crysoprase, Prase

TOOLS Rain Pipe

HERBS Skullcap

MATERIALS Coral, Water

ANIMALS Beetle, Crab, Duck, Fish, Osprey, Scorpion, Turtle, Water Snakes, Llorelei, Nymphs, Undines

PLANTS Alder, Kelp, Mangrove, Watercress

SIGIL

The Wave or Cyclic Kala is as subtle and powerful as the water it is named for. Enchantments, glamours and illusions should all be worked with this Kala. Works of dissolution, to dissolve existing form, may also benefit from the use of this Kala. The Wave Kala may also be used to encourage visions during fasting prior to magickal workings or for prolonged trance dance magicks.

Divination by skrying in liquids may also benefit from the use of this Kala, which may be used to consecrate and charge both the container and the fluid being used for skrying. The Wave Kala is good for sealing a space, magick often has a problem crossing running water due to its fluid ever-changing nature, and this Kala reflects this. Hence it also works for absorbing negativity as well.

The Strength Kala

CORRESPONDS:	Earth
MAGICKS	Divination by Casting, Geomancy, Psychometry, Strength Magick, Terramancy
SYMBOL	Disk
COLOUR	Yellow
SCENTS	Patchouli
CRYSTALS	Magnetite, Marble, Onyx, Soapstone
TOOLS	Club, Pentacle
HERBS	Coltsfoot
MATERIALS	Earth, Salt, Sand, Stone, Wood
ANIMALS	Bull, Deer, Hedgehog, Ostritch, Rhea, Dryads, Fauns, Gnomes, Minotaurs
PLANTS	Barley, Bramble, Daisy, Flax, Millet, Narcissus, Orchis, Potato, Yarrow

SIGIL

The Ground or Strength Kala is good for enhancing physical based magicks. Forms of divination like geomancy or those involving casting, like the Runes or I Ching may also be enhanced through its use. Magicks to enhance physical strength and endurance may also benefit from use of this Kala, including martial arts.

Other works that one would classically perform with the element of Earth may also be worked with this Kala.

The Transformation Kala

CORRESPONDS :	Fire
MAGICKS	Purification, Pyromancy, Transformation
SYMBOL	Wand
COLOUR	Red
SCENTS	Labdanum, Olibanum
CRYSTALS	Carnelian, Fire Opal, Orange Calcite, Serpentine
TOOLS	Axe, Rattle, Sistrum, Torch
HERBS	Betel, Ephedra, Guarana
MATERIALS	Fire, Sulphur
ANIMALS	Desert Lizards, Serpent, Phoenix, Salamanders
PLANTS	Cactus, Geranium, Hibiscus, Red Poppy, Tiger Lily

SIGIL

The Flame or Transformation Kala is a powerful tool for changing the self. Work with this Kala if you are undergoing any therapy or counseling, or dealing with baggage. Other forms of purification and transformation are also very effective with this Kala.

It is also a good Kala to use in preparation for major magickal operations. Fire magicks such as skrying in the flames or summoning may also be enhanced through the use of this Kala.

The Breath Kala

CORRESPONDS:	Air
MAGICKS	Aeromancy, Clairaudience, Divination by Image, Intuitive Magicks
SYMBOL	Dagger
COLOUR	Sky Blue
SCENTS	Dammar, Galbanum
CRYSTALS	Alexandrite, Blue Calcite, Chalcedony, Iceland Spar, Jacinth
TOOLS	Bag, Censer, Fan, Flute
HERBS	Cannabis
MATERIALS	Feather, Glass
ANIMALS	Antelope, Chameleon, Dragonfly, Gazelle, Man, Swallow, Apparitions, Banshee, Fairie, Harpies, Pegasus, Sylphs
PLANTS	Aspen, Verbena

SIGIL

The Breath Kala or Wind Kala is used for magicks that sharpen and utilize the mental faculties. As with the other elemental Kalas, it can be produced through any form of sexual activity. Control of the breath is an important tool of the magician, and so this Kala should be used in combination with pranayama. It may be used for healing work with the throat and lungs. You may also consecrate image divinatory tools like Tarot and Runes with this Kala.

Intuition being one of the most important tools of the magician, this Kala should also be used to sharpen your intuition, being charged and consumed specifically for this purpose. Trusting the intuition is an important step in magickal growth, and you must learn to always trust that gut feeling, it is never wrong, the mistakes come when you try and rationalize it away.

The Spirit Kala

CORRESPONDS :   Spirit

MAGICKS   Alignment with Divinity

SYMBOL   Winged Egg or Serpent surrounded Egg

COLOUR   All

CRYSTALS   Diamond

SIGIL

The Spirit Kala can be seen as the elixir vitae of the alchemists. It is the Philosopher's Stone, the ultimate magickal elixir. As such it can only be produced by the combination of the red lion and the white eagle, i.e. priest and priestess when she is red. This is well expressed by the Art card in the Thoth tarot deck. To produce this Kala would be the result of perfect conditions, perfect state of mind and perfect union, so it is the goal to be strived for. It is the height for which we all strive. This Kala corresponds to the Tao, the indwelling Essence of All, and as such could be considered the force of life and of soul-stuff.

If you are combining more than one Kala to gain the benefits of the different energies, you may choose to combine the symbols of the Kalas for sigils. Alternatively, if using at least three Kalas, you may prefer to use the symbol below, the MetaKala sigil.

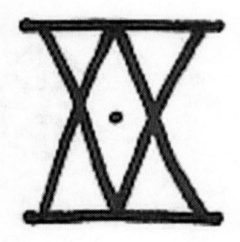

13　Kundalini Rising

Coiled at the base of the spine at the Muladhara chakra is the Kundalini, perceived as a serpent coiled three and a half times. "Kundali" means "spiral", which is significant in light of the coiling - for the DNA double helix repeats every 3.5 A° (angstroms or 10-10m), and of course the double serpents on the caduceus cross three and a half times.

The symbolism of the caduceus depicting the subtle body is unmistakeable on examination. The straight wand is the Sushumna [spinal energy channel], containing the six "main" chakras as far as Ajna, with the criss-crossing Ida and Pingala channels forming the serpents. The winged disk on the top is the ajna chakra, with its two nadis or petals, depicted as wings. These highly suggestive correspondences emphasise the interconnection, both symbolic and actual, of the subtle body with the physical body.

When the kundalini is sufficiently energised and roused to rise, it ascends through the chakras. Some western writers erroneously claim that it can cause madness if it does not reach the crown chakra, or that it gets stuck. As the kundalini is preparing to rise, feelings of intense heat may be felt, and profuse sweating often occurs; bodily twitches and involuntary spasms may also occur before and during the ascent; senses become hypersensitive.

When I have had kundalini experiences created by non-sexual methods I have found them less easy to retain any sort of bodily control with. This may sound strange, as you cannot really retain control when your kundalini rises, you have to go with the flow. What I mean is that kundalini experiences generated by for example combining psychedelics in quantity with vigorous dancing tends (in my experience) to result in the body fainting and falling over, whereas kundalini experiences generated by love-making tend to leave the body on automatic pilot while your consciousness is transformed and soars.

Describing kundalini experience is very difficult, language, as is often the case, being inadequate to the task. The experience tends to vary depending on how high the kundalini ascends.

If any of your chakras are not in balance with the others, and this only needs to be by a small amount, the kundalini is unlikely to rise past that chakra. Instead, an experience appropriate to that chakra is likely; when you regain sufficient awareness of your body and are not totally blissed out, the remaining energy can be directed to balancing out the unbalanced chakra.

The descriptions below are based on my experiences, other people may and will have different perceptions of these, I am merely trying to indicate how these stages have been in my being to encourage contemplation of this phenomena. I have found that in all cases there is a sense of bliss which is far beyond orgasm, becoming even more intense as the kundalini rises higher.

To the Crown - produces total bliss, samadhi, oneness with the universe, whatever you want to call it. The fire serpent Goddess has risen, woken the passive God to dance and the nectar of purity and perfection rains back down the body, yin and yang conjoined. The experience of being everything, infinite and all-encompassing, is beyond belief, beyond dreams.

To the Third Eye - produces oneness with the universe, with a perception of the myriad planes, intertwined, overlaying, energies and resonances, the fabric of existence or Web of Wyrd visible and showing the interconnectedness of all things, the absence of subject and object. The experience of the wonder and pricelessness of life for its own sake, the value of each and every thing.

To the Throat - produces oneness with the microcosm of the self, expanded into the macrocosm, experience of the body of the Star Goddess, combination of the senses and faculties to remove any doubt, the experience which destroys any doubt and destroys faith - faith becomes experience and being.

To the Heart - produces a feeling of universal love and compassion, a sense of balance and strengthening of the will, as meaning and purpose are reinforced. Could perhaps be called the experience of the Bodhisattva.

To the Solar Plexus - produces a strengthening and refinement of the emotions, an enhanced appreciation of your environment, both people and places. Enhances the aura and the senses. Deepens love for lovers, friends and family.

To the Sacral Centre - produces a strengthening of the body, including the immune system.

To the Base of the Spine - produces a sexual delight, encourages Kala production, enhances the immediate experience.

14　KiaLiaMiaNiaSia – The Mantra of Becoming

In 1987 I discussed mantras with a friend and working partner, Grey Fox, and the creation of mantras by allowing barbarous words of power to surface from the unconscious mind when in a state of gnosis. We both agreed that Spare's term Kia was a very effective mantra, and would make a good starting point from which to produce other mantras.

After about an hour of mantra, I suddenly realized an obvious sequence of mantric words from the root Kia we were using, bellowed KiaLiaMiaNiaSia, at which Grey Fox froze into total silence and immobility and stared at me. After a very long pregnant pause, he asked me in hushed tones what I had just said. I repeated the word and he insisted I write it down and start analyzing it immediately as it seemed very significant.

The mantra seemed to have a life of its own, and as I repeated it to him, I realized the mantra was a progression on the primal magickal root Ia, starting at Kia, which begins with K (Kaph) through the next four letters of the Hebrew alphabet, i.e. L (Lamed), M (Mem), N (Nun) and S (Samekh) - earlier

Qabalistic training resurfacing, perhaps. Closer analysis and subsequent work revealed this simple sequence to be extremely powerful and effective as a working tool.

My first reaction after I had uttered this sequence was to analyse what I had said. The sequence of 15 letters, with a recurring root and 5 constituent parts seemed to offer all sorts of possibilities, which have been justified.

For people who do not like gematria and analysis of numbers, I will try and keep it to a realistic minimum, but it is relevant in showing the power of language as structural form in directing the sounds (transmutable energy) uttered by the magician. As the Tantriks say:

Mantra + Yantra = Tantra
Force + Form = Action/Expansion

The mantra KiaLiaMiaNiaSia is based on the root mantra Ia, the primal word of magick, (which adds to eleven, the number of magick) which is the base of each of the five constituent parts. The five root mantras Kia, Lia, Mia, Nia, Sia have the values of 31, 41, 51, 61, 71 respectively. The gematria is using the Hebrew alphabet and corresponding numerical values.

All of these mantras sum to prime numbers apart from the central word Mia, which breaks down to the factors of 3 and 17. By its very sound, and without having to use any imagination, we equated Mia to the Mother as the generative principle, or that which can divide from itself.

Nia was equated to the Daughter, as that is its meaning in Hebrew. Lia became the Father, 41 also equalling GAVAL, "Divine Majesty". This left Sia as the Son, Kia being Spirit, akin to Shin with its Spirit attribution when added to IHVH to form IHShVH.

Hence the sequence is Spirit, Father, Mother, Daughter, Son, although we tend to find the former and latter pairs both fairly interchangeable at times. Adding the values of the different letters in the word, i.e. K, I, A, L, M, N, S produces 211, another prime.

At the time I wondered why the sequence stopped at Sia, so I noted down what continuing the sequence would produce. The next mantra is OLA, which does not flow with the others, and adds to 81 (non-prime, though the square of nine and fourth power of three) thus introducing another non-prime.

Rearranging the letters gives the word IAO, another of the classic power words. However IAO can also have the value of 17 (taking the O as Vav), a root of Mia and of the mantra as a whole (the total of the mantra is $255 = 15 \times 17$), so its influence is still felt in the mantra.

The previous mantra would be IIA with a value of 21 (again non-prime, factors 3 and 7), which also does not flow with the sequence, and introduces duplication of letters within the root. So the sequence produced from my unconscious in the state of gnosis was the ONLY sequence of five words that could be produced with the required levels of power inherent in it.

As well as equating the five root mantras to the members of the divine family, there are obvious correlations such as to the elements and Kalas which needed investigating. The most obvious correlation was the 15 letters to the 15 Kalas, supported by the first four letters, which rearrange to produce - KALI, the Great Goddess from whose Yoni the Kalas flow.

From an elemental viewpoint, Kia corresponds to Spirit (viz. Spare's concept of the Neither-Neither). Interestingly, Kia equals 31, as does HVK, "to go", the fifth and most important part of the magickal axiom - To Know, To Will, To Dare, To Keep Silent. Lia equals 41, as does GChL, "to burn", so Fire seemed an obvious attribution (the letters of the root LIA, i.e. A, I, L, can be found in at least half of the power names in Hebrew such as Archangels and Divine Names.

Mia equals 51, same as AKL "to eat", so Earth was attributed. Nia had water attributed by a process of elimination, as Sia adds to 71, same value as INVH and IVNH, both meaning "a dove", and CIiZVN, "a vision, apparition", giving Air attributions. (For anyone of a Typhonian bent, 71, being Air or Space, would be expected to have ETs attributed to it, and sure enough, LAM equals 71).

As for me this mantra embodied the concept of action, I called it the Mantra of Becoming. From this came the inspiration for this book, the magick of becoming, or becoming magick. For it is vital as magicians that we do not forget the fifth element and its formula. Having worked through the elements and developed the qualities – To Know, To Will, To Dare and To Keep Silent, we must combine these in balance to make the quintessence, Spirit, whose quality is To Go or Become.

Analysis with the Kalas
The first thing I noticed on analyzing KiaLiaMiaNiaSia using the Prime Qabalah (PQ) was that it totals to the same number, 255, as it does in Hebrew. It also totals to 255 in Greek Qabalah (taking alpha =1, iota = 10, kappa = 20, lambda = 30, mu = 40, nu = 5-, sigma = 60). This synchronicity demonstrates that this word is extremely magickally significant

as its number is the same in three systems, something I have not discovered for any other such words.

I decided to attribute the fifteen letters of KiaLiaMiaNiaSia to the fifteen Kalas, in the same way that fifteen of the sixteen (nitya)Kalas are attributed to the Srividya (Supreme Science) mantra. This then gives five magickal formulae involving the Kala energies. The sixteenth Kala is then attributed to the source of life. From this came the inspiration for the Mass of the Feather and Scale. I have not found any other numbers in the Prime Qabalah yet that add to the same as KiaLiaMiaNiaSia, but the ideas generated demonstrate the value of this formula.

Use of parts of the mantra as roots has also proven to be very effective in conjunction with other techniques, as detailed in the chapter on Nightside Squares. KiaLiaMiaNiaSia also makes a very powerful spinning mantra for use in Mantra webs.

The Kalas as depicted in the Kali Yantra and the Mantra of Becoming

Web   K

Knowledge   △ of Magickal Awareness   I

Sorcery   A

Energy		L
Love	△ of Spiritual Growth	I
Will		A
Strength		M
Devotion	△ of Grace and Right Action	I
Nature		A
Cyclic		N
Transformation	△ of The Mysterious Female,	I
Breath	or △ of The Cycle of True Breath	A
Tidal		S
Time	△ of Force and Form	I
Space		A
Spirit	• of Life and Essence	O

These attributions give five formulas for the five parts of the Mantra of Becoming:

KIA - The Web of Knowledge and Sorcery
LIA - The Energy of Love and Will
MIA - The Strength of Devotion to Nature
NIA - The Cyclic Transformation of Breath
SIA - The Tides of Time and Space

David Rankine

15   The Mass of the Feather and the Scale

Gas vios emmi kai ouranou asteroentos   Hum
Let earth be still
Ra
Let water be still   Ma
Let fire be still   Da
Let air be still   Sa
Let aether be still   Se
Let me fly on the wings of intent   So
Let thought become action   Hung
KiaLiaMiaNiaSia

I stand in magickal awareness, in the web of knowledge and
sorcery   Kia

I strive for spiritual growth, through the energy of love and will
                                                Lia

I become through grace and right action, manifesting the
strength of devotion to nature   Mia

I sustain through the mysterious female, expressing the cyclic transformation of breath   Nia

I embody force and form, riding the tides of time and space.
                                                         Sia

In the sphere I am everywhere the centre   Agapé

I am the magician and the exorcist, I dwell in the void place of spirit, palace of kings and queens

There are four gates to the palace
They are of:

Silver	Iao	(face E)
Gold	Lashtal	(face S)
Stones of precious water	Ipsos	(face W)
Ultimate sparks of the intimate fire	Gea	(face N)

There are eight spokes on the wheel

Vitriol	(NE)
Azoth	(E)
Al	(SE)
Thelema	(S)
La	(SW)
Lux	(W)
Ka	(NW)
Nox	(N)
And it spins between heaven	Ia (above)
And the underworld	Aum (below)

I am pure will, true of intent and thus perfect being
Desireless, I see the mysteries
Desiring, I create their manifestation

Remember all ye that existence is pure joy, the joy of the silver stars: that all the sorrows are but as shadows; they pass and are done, but there is that which remains.

KiaLiaMiaNiaSia

Analysis of the Mass of the Feather and the Scale

This ritual is a crystallization of much of the work contained elsewhere in this book. I created it as a ritual of alignment with the energies of the Aeon of Maat (i.e. Truth).

Although the ritual should be performed without long pauses, for convenience and to clarify the nature of the ritual you will notice that it is divided into five sections. Each of these five sections is considered below with explanations of corresponding actions and visualisations.

The first part of the Mass can be seen as the magician identifying him/herself with the elements on a cosmic scale, and balancing their energies in him/herself.

The ritual begins with I am a child of earth and starry heaven – the Greek oath from the Orphic mysteries affirming the identity of the magician as a combination of the elements. This is followed by lines from a C2-3 Coptic magickal papyri (the sequence from Let earth be still through to Let aether be still), and can be seen as the sequence of elements moving from the most solid through to the most subtle.

As the first part links the magician as the focus of his/her personal universe with the energies that flow through the universe, the mantras for the chakras are also vibrated to energise the body and to reinforce the link. The mantra for the feet chakra (Hum) opens the link between the magician and the earth below.

Whilst these lines and the corresponding mantras are intoned, the hands should form the appropriate mudras in front of each chakra, moving up in turn with the flow of sound.

When the third eye chakra is reached we move beyond the five elements. The element of light is associated with this chakra, so the wave flow of energy directed by intent is emphasised.

At the crown the magician declares the unity of thought and deed, the aim of perfect action where there is no delay between the thought and the consequent action.

Next is the invocation of the energy of Maat with the Mantra of Becoming, to emphasise and invoke the energies of all the different currents the Kalas represent, as mentioned in the analysis of KiaLiaMiaNiaSia in the previous chapter.

The second section focuses the energies of the Kalas into an energy Yantra/web around the magician using the formulae of these energies.

The magician identifies with the fifteen Kalas in five statements, which correspond to the five triangles of the Kali Yantra. I have named each triangle to emphasise the link with different magickal formulae. These formulae are all aspects of the magician's worldview - magickal awareness, spiritual growth, grace and right action, the mysterious female (the divine feminine as the creative force, also hinting at the power of shakti and kundalini), and force and form.

The three sides of each triangle equate to three of the Kalas, which are named in the second part of the statement. Hence web, knowledge and sorcery; energy, love and will; strength, devotion and nature; cyclic, transformation and breath; tidal, time and space.

The magician should visualize five concentric red equilateral triangles point down (to the south) around him/herself, starting at the inner and working to the outer. The mantra of Becoming is likewise identified with the Kala formulae and the 5 triangles of the Kali Yantra.

The focus then returns to the magician, who is identifying with the bindu or point in the centre of the Kali Yantra and seeing him/herself as such. The line from Liber Al II.3 (In the sphere I am everywhere the centre) identifies the magician with the concept of Hadit, the point at the centre of the sphere, i.e. that s/he is the centre of their own magickal universe. The Kala mantra for Venus, which corresponds to the centre of the sphere, is intoned to emphasise this statement.

The third section continues the formation of the Kali Yantra, through the visualization of the four gates of the Yantra being identified with the four elements. It also brings the elemental energies into balance and reinforces the astral temple sphere about the magician.

This section begins with the combination of part of AL II.7 (I am the magician and the exorcist), the concept of the void as the place of unmanifest potential (as described in Liber Samekh), and the idea of the palace as described in AL I.51. The palace is being used as an analogy to the temple, indicating the nobility of a true magician who acts for the good of all. This section emphasises the creation of the astral temple space and its alignment with the flow of Maatian energy through the universe.

The ritual continues with another line from AL I.51 (There are four gates to the palace) to describe the elemental attributions used as the standard interface around the sphere. The four elemental gates correspond to the four gates on the Kali Yantra. I have identified these with the ordeals described in AL II.64-67 (silver, gold, stones of precious water and ultimate sparks of the intimate fire).

The Kala mantras for the four elements are also intoned, balancing the power of the flow of the elements through the centre of the sphere. Whilst these mantras are intoned the mudras for the elements should also be made with the hands, though this time they should all be in front of the heart as the centre of balance to demonstrate the harmony achieved.

The fourth section moves to the planetary energies, linking the eight petals of the Kali Yantra to the eight spokes on the Wheel of Time, also known as the Wheel of the Year, and the eight planets attributed around the sphere. The eight petals of the Kali Yantra are visualized (as purple for the spiritual energies) and the planetary energies brought into balance as the planetary Kala mantras are intoned.

Once this is done the magician establishes the axis mundi by describing the stars above and underworld below. As the Kala mantras are intoned the magician should direct his/her gaze first up and then down. Essentially the magician is now expanding their boundaries from within the Yantra to become the universe. S/he affirms their identity as the axis mundi in the Wheel of Time, and so outside the constraints of mundane reality.

The final section affirms the purity of intent of the magician, emphasising the alignment with the Maatian current of truth and order. The formula of no desire/desire describes the action of magickal intent. There can be no desire to successfully achieve, for this can hinder the intent, but conversely when the intent is clear, then it must be powered by the will, and the desire is part of the force that feeds the will to achieve the intent.

A final statement declares the bliss of unity with all – emphasising the interconnectedness of everything. This is described by the slightly modified line from AL II.9 (*Remember all ye .. that which remains*), which has been made more stellar and universal in its implications by the addition of the line *the joy of the silver stars*.

The rite ends with an affirmation of alignment with the energies of the Aeon of Maat, with Truth, by intoning again the Mantra of Becoming, also earthing the energies through to radiate into mundane existence.

David Rankine

16   Eating Your Words –
Magickal Ingestion

This chapter was inspired by my research into Heka, the magick practiced by the ancient Egyptians to facilitate their daily lives. When we perform magick, we usually think of our words working outside our body, and the sound energy vibrating at particular frequencies to achieve particular effects. The power of such techniques through mantra, intonation of Divine Names and sacred languages is undeniable. However the other side of the breath, as it were, is often ignored. So let us consider the benefits of taking the words into our bodies in different ways.

One technique used by the ancient Egyptians was to write the required spell on a piece of virgin papyrus. The papyrus would then be dissolved in beer and be consumed with a drink of water to take the power of the spell and the words into the body. This technique is an ideal one to use for healing work, taking the magick physically into the body to continue its action from within to without. Obviously you could choose a different base than beer, and use paper or parchment, but this is an area to experiment with before performing the magick!

Another common technique was the use of a magickal ink made from myrrh and morning dew. The spell would be written on the skin to create an effect on one level. The words would then be licked off, combining the magickal power of the saliva with the words and the ink in the mouth (an Egyptian name for magick was "the art of the mouth"). The ink and saliva would then be swallowed and continue to act from within the body. Myrrh was ideal to use, as it has no negative effects on the body, and indeed is anti-fungicidal and anti-bacterial so its ingestion had practical medicinal virtues as well. This technique seems to logically lend itself to the use of sigils on the body to be absorbed within.

A third technique used by Egyptian magicians that also holds great appeal for modern magickal work generally was the use of the feather of Maat. The feather of Maat would be drawn on the tongue with a magickal ink before performing ritual to ensure that the magician spoke only words of truth which upheld the natural harmony of the universe. In modern terms we can equate that with Will-driven magick rather than Ego-driven magick.

A technique I have adapted from the writings of the Christian mystic Hildegard von Bingen is the use of crystals to create sigils on food you have made, especially bread. If you are making sacramental food, from cakes of light to cookies to bread, then why not empower it by using an appropriate (to the nature of the rite) crystal to mark a sigil or intent onto the food. Likewise food colourings could be used to create yantras, mandalas or sigils onto food you have bought or prepared.

A technique I have developed works if you are a smoker who uses roll-ups. Tobacco has a long history of sacramental use, and can be used in a ritual context for working with spirits.

This technique can be used for this, and also for other purposes as will become apparent. When you make your roll-up using tobacco (or other herbs such as coltsfoot or passion flower would also work), add a small cardboard filter at the end you inhale from (a "roach"). Before placing the filter in, write your intent or a sigil on the cardboard, so that the smoke passes over it as you inhale.

As with the ink, you are then inhaling smoke which is charged with the intent you have written on the filter. I appreciate this technique will not appeal to everyone, especially non-smokers, but I am attempting to present ideas here for consideration and to encourage a perception shift in the way you approach magick!

David Rankine

17 The Trans-Uranian Magick Squares

The kameas have been used as a basis for talismans and creating sigils for centuries. However, since the discovery of Uranus, Neptune and Pluto, nobody has come up with kameas for these planets. To correct this omission, I decided to create new ones for these planets.

It is not feasible to have a magick square that is less than 3x3, and 3x3 through to 9x9 are taken for the seven classical planets. As these are numbered by Qabalistic attribution, I decided to start in the same vein. I also decided with the change in perception relating to the Earth and Her energies, that a kamea for planet Earth is appropriate.

Thus the first of my suggested attributions, starting with qabalistic attributions, is 10x10 for Earth (Malkuth). Likewise 11 as the number of magick and Daath is associated with Uranus, so this planet has an 11x11 magick square.

Neptune and Pluto are a bit trickier, so I opted for a simple approach, i.e. keep moving away from the centre in order.

Neptune is the next planet out from the centre of our universe after Uranus, so I assigned the 12x12 square to Neptune. The 13x13 square for Pluto follows the same principle.

I followed the same mathematical formula used for the classical kameas to formulate the additional kameas I suggest for use here.

Sigilisation with the Kameas

I include the classic method of creating sigils using the kameas here for the convenience of the reader.

The standard method of creating sigils on the kameas uses Hebrew letters, and the Aiq Beker square (which takes its name from the letters attributed to the first two numbers, i.e. aleph, yod, qoph – AIQ, then beth, kaph, resh – BKR). This system reduces the numbers attributed to the letters to a numerical value in the range 1-9, ignoring the zeros of tens and hundreds.

1	2	3
Aleph (1) Yod (10) Qoph (100)	Beth (2) Kaph (20) Resh (200)	Gimel (3) Lamed (30) Shin (300)
4	5	6
Daleth (4) Mem (40) Tau (400)	He (5) Nun (50) Final Kaph (500)	Vau (6) Samekh (60) Final Mem (600)
7	8	9
Zain (7) Ayin (70) Final Nun (700)	Cheth (8) Pe (80) Final Pe (800)	Teth (9) Tzaddi (90) Final Tzaddi (900)

The sigil is always begun with a small circle in the middle of the square the first letter is attributed to. This is joined by a straight line to the middle of the square the next letter is in. This process is repeated until the line is drawn to the middle of the square to which the last letter is attributed, where a small cross-bar is drawn to end the sigil.

If two consecutive letters are attributed to the same box in the kamea, this is indicated by a small loop. If a third or fourth letter were also attributed to the same box, an extra loop is added for each extra letter in the word that has the same numerical attribution.

Two examples of this technique
Azrael is written AZRAL in Hebrew.
A + Z + R + A + L
1 + 7 + 200 + 1 + 30 = 239
Using Aiq Beker, the sigil will be represented by the sequence
1 − 7 − 2 − 1 − 3
If we draw this on say the Saturn kamea, we get the following sigil.

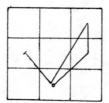

If however we were to draw the sigil for a word where there is are more than one consecutive number of the same value, such as Satariel, the Qliphoth of Binah (hence appropriate for the Saturnian kamea), it would give the sequence 6 − 1 − 4 − 1 − 2 − 1 − 1 − 3, i.e. Samekh = 6(0), Aleph = 1, Tau = 4(00),

Aleph = 1, Resh = 2(00), Yod = 1(0), Aleph = 1, Lamed = 3(0).

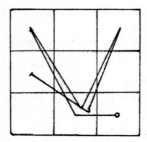

Now if you want to work with the English language, the 1-9 system may be attributed to the letters of the alphabet working systematically through. Another option is to use the Prime Qabalah. For the new suggested squares, the reduction principle is not needed, as they contain all the primes under 100 in them, so the sigil could be created using the Prime Qabalah attributions wholesale with these squares.

Earth

10	92	3	97	5	96	94	8	99	1
11	19	83	14	86	85	17	88	12	90
80	22	28	74	25	26	77	23	79	71
31	69	33	37	65	66	34	68	62	40
51	42	58	44	46	45	57	53	49	60
50	52	48	54	56	55	47	43	59	41
61	39	63	67	36	35	64	38	32	70
30	72	78	27	75	76	24	73	29	21
81	89	18	84	16	15	87	13	82	20
100	9	93	7	95	6	4	98	2	91

New Kameas for the Trans-Uranian Planets

Uranus

56	117	46	107	36	97	26	87	16	77	6
7	57	118	47	108	37	98	27	88	17	67
68	8	58	119	48	109	38	99	28	78	18
19	69	9	59	120	49	110	39	89	29	79
80	20	70	10	60	121	50	100	40	90	30
31	81	21	71	11	61	111	51	101	41	91
92	32	82	22	72	1	62	112	52	102	42
43	93	33	83	12	73	2	63	113	53	103
104	44	94	23	84	13	74	3	64	114	54
55	105	34	95	24	85	14	75	4	65	115
116	45	106	35	96	25	86	15	76	5	66

Neptune

12	134	135	5	4	138	139	8	9	142	143	1
121	23	22	128	129	19	18	124	125	15	14	132
109	34	34	116	117	31	30	112	113	27	26	120
48	98	99	41	40	102	103	45	44	106	107	37
60	86	87	53	52	90	91	57	56	94	95	49
73	71	70	80	81	67	66	76	77	63	62	84
61	83	82	69	69	79	78	64	65	75	74	72
96	50	51	89	88	54	55	93	92	58	59	85
108	38	39	101	100	42	43	105	104	46	47	97
25	119	118	32	33	115	114	28	29	111	110	36
13	131	130	20	21	127	126	16	17	123	122	24
144	2	3	137	136	6	7	141	140	10	11	133

Pluto

79	164	67	152	55	140	43	128	31	116	19	104	7
8	80	165	68	153	56	141	44	129	32	117	20	92
93	9	81	166	69	154	57	142	45	130	33	105	21
22	94	10	82	167	70	155	58	143	46	118	34	106
107	23	95	11	83	168	71	156	59	131	47	119	35
36	108	24	96	12	84	169	72	144	60	132	48	120
121	37	109	25	97	13	85	157	73	145	61	133	49
50	122	38	110	26	98	1	86	158	74	146	62	134
135	51	123	39	111	14	99	2	87	159	75	147	63
64	136	52	124	27	112	15	100	3	88	160	76	148
149	65	137	40	125	28	113	16	101	4	89	161	77
78	150	53	138	41	126	29	114	17	102	5	90	162
163	66	151	54	139	42	127	30	115	18	103	6	91

The Classical Planetary Kameas

Saturn

4	9	2
3	5	7
8	1	6

Jupiter

4	14	15	1
9	7	6	12
5	11	10	8
16	2	3	13

Mars

11	24	7	20	3
4	12	25	8	16
17	5	13	21	9
10	18	1	14	22
23	6	19	2	15

Sun

6	32	3	34	35	1
7	11	27	28	8	30
19	14	16	15	23	24
18	20	22	21	17	13
25	29	10	9	26	12
36	5	33	4	2	31

Venus

22	47	16	41	10	35	4
5	23	48	17	42	11	29
30	6	24	49	18	36	12
13	31	7	25	43	19	37
38	14	32	1	26	44	20
21	39	8	33	2	27	45
46	15	40	9	34	3	28

Mercury

8	58	59	5	4	62	63	1
49	15	14	52	53	11	10	56
41	23	22	44	48	19	18	45
32	34	35	29	25	38	39	28
40	26	27	37	36	30	31	33
17	47	46	20	21	43	42	24
9	55	54	12	13	51	50	16
64	2	3	61	60	6	7	57

Moon

37	78	29	70	21	62	13	54	5
6	38	79	30	71	22	63	14	46
47	7	39	80	31	72	23	55	15
16	48	8	40	81	32	64	24	56
57	17	49	9	41	73	33	65	25
26	58	18	50	1	42	74	34	66
67	27	59	10	51	2	43	75	35
36	68	19	60	11	52	3	44	76
77	28	69	20	61	12	53	4	45

David Rankine

18   On Creating Thought Forms

Thought forms (also known as elementaries or such elaborate terms as chao-servitors) are created by the will through visualisation. Their purpose is to carry out a set task determined by the operator(s). Thought forms can be created to accomplish any manner of task, and may have any form, but the form should be sympathetic to the task, and the task of realistic proportion.

When this type of thought form is created it should be named and given a lifespan, dissolving back into its constituent elements at the end of its lifespan. General tasks should not be set, precision is required in creating a thought form and setting its task, e.g. heal X of condition Y within a specified time.

As with sigils, thought forms should be forgotten about after creation. Energy of the appropriate Kala(s) should be used in the formation e.g. Will, Energy, Love, etc. The thought form should be given the necessary skills to achieve its task, e.g. ability to locate a specified person, ability to heal, etc, and these abilities should be named during the creation.

If a thought form is to have a long life span (beyond a few lunar months), it may be attached to a physical object, such as a crystal, talisman, statue, etc or housed in a spirit bottle or jar.

Creation

The exact form, lifespan, name, skills and task should be determined precisely. The operator(s) should sit (in a circle if more than one) and visualise it in the centre of the sphere. The direction the thought form is facing should also have been pre-determined, so that if there is more than one operator they see the appropriate view (side, front, back).

The function and abilities should be stated and willed into the thought form, and the lifespan and name stated. The abilities should be repeated mentally by the operator(s) as a mantra whilst visualising the thought form performing its task.

The order should then be given to the thought form, stated clearly and concisely as it is sent to perform its task e.g. "Grimalkin, you will go forth, find X and give her the energy and clear headedness she needs to pass her driving test. You have one week to perform this task, after which you will return to the elements from which you came".

As the order is given a visualisation of the desired result should be given to the thought form to ensure it understands the task it has been set.

19   Making Misery
        Magickal

This chapter was written during a severe attack of the flu in 1991, and deals with the pragmatic use of what are often seen as "negative" states of being. However, the energies involved in serious illness and grief may be used productively. One of the signs of a good magician (in my opinion) is this ability to turn negative events around to positive ones and transform the situation to your advantage.

When ill with the flu or any other illness strong enough to knock you into bed, you are in an ideal position to take advantage of the fever dream. You can explore the astral realities through either projection (the phenomena of astral projection in relation to illness is well-documented, but see *Shamanism* by Mircea Eliade for an excellent account of the uses of illness by shamans) or by skrying the fever dream.

I have found sustained pranayama (if not prevented by a congested nose) a good aid to achieving the state of gnosis sometimes necessary to achieve these visions. Skullcap tea also helps with the lucidity of the visions when in the twilight realms of half sleep/fever dream. If you do have a congested nose, try reciting a mantra inaudibly, or better still, set up several artificial personalities and spin a mantra between them, until the disorientation helps lift your vision.

As the throat is often affected by the bugs that force you into bed, and the Vishuddha or throat chakra is the centre of dreaming, I usually focus a lot of my personal energy on my throat when I am ill. This has the double purpose of helping focus more lucidly on astral visions, and also means my throat is fit to be used for raising energies sooner.

The death of a loved one is never pleasant, but most of our grief comes from selfishness, therefore it seems logical to focus that selfish energy on transforming the self positively rather than disintegrate it. In 1986 a lady I loved very much was killed in an accident. I was like a zombie for months until one day I was reading my bible, the *Tao Teh King*, and I realised my selfishness and then because aware of what time of year was approaching - Samhain.

At Samhain, I went to Binsey Well in Oxford, a local power spot that is known traditionally as a gate to the underworld, and from there I embarked on an astral journey. On my return, I was transformed. My journey had been successful, and I had realized that transitory dance of Chaos we all spin.

From this point my whole magickal directions changed in a very positive dynamic fashion, and I developed my own system of sorcery. Since that Samhain I have lost other friends, to old age, in accidents and to Artificially Induced Death Syndrome, but now my sadness is more transient and my steps unfaltering.

Extreme emotional and physical states are extremely powerful
energy sources to be tapped when available for self-evolution,
so don't let patterns imposed on you by others affect your
thinking (if they're self-imposed, so be it.)

David Rankine

Appendix 1 - A List of P.Q. Attributions

Prime Qabalah Dictionary

A	1	H	29	O	5	U	7
B	11	I	3	P	53	V	73
C	13	J	31	Q	59	W	79
D	17	K	37	R	61	X	83
E	2	L	41	S	67	Y	89
F	19	M	43	T	71	Z	97
G	23	N	47				

No.	Properties	Factors	Word
1	1^2, 1!, P		A
2	2!, P		E
3	Σ2, P		I
4	2^2	2	IA
5	P		Elements O
6	3!, Σ3	2, 3	AO
7	P		Classic Planets Colours of the Rainbow Days of the Week
8	2^3	2, 4	Trigrams of the I Ching Io
9	3^2	3	Gates in the Circle Worlds in Norse Myth Planets IAO
10	Σ4	2, 5	
11	P		The Number of Magick Astrological Planets
12		2, 3, 4, 6	Signs of the Zodiac
13	P		Lunar Months
14		2, 7	
15	Σ5	3, 5	Bee
16	$4^2=2^4$	2, 4, 8	Chandra-Kalas Ace
17	P		
18		2, 3, 6, 9	Ice
19	P		
20		2, 4, 5, 10	
21	Σ6	3, 7	Aid
22		2, 11	Hebrew Letters, Major Arcana
23	P		

53	P		
54		2, 3, 6, 9, 18, 27	NU One
55	Σ10	5, 11	And Aeon
56		2, 4, 7, 8, 14, 28	Pi
57		3, 19	Lace
58		2, 29	Book
59	P		DAGDA Mace
60		2, 3, 4, 5, 6, 10, 12, 15, 20, 30	
61	P		Blue Lead Mad
62		2, 31	
63		3, 7, 9, 21	Aback
64	$8^2=4^3=2^6$	2, 4, 8, 16, 32	*Hexagrams of the I Ching* Ear
65		5, 13	Air Life
66	Σ11	2, 3, 6, 11, 22, 33	Leg
67	P		Dome
68		2, 4, 17, 34	Bible Gem
69		3, 23	BADBH Eagle
70		2, 5, 7, 10, 14, 35	Aura Doom Fool Is Sea
71	P		ISA Peace
72		2, 3, 4, 6, 8, 9, 12, 18, 24, 36	*Names of God in the Shemhamphorash* ODIN Image
73	P		Cup Heal Khu
74		2, 37	AGNI Deep Game
75		3, 5, 15, 25	Bare Bear Bough

24	4!	2, 3, 4, 6, 8, 12	*Greek Letters, Runes* Of
25	5^2	5	Babe
26		2, 13	*English Letters* Age
27	3^3	3, 9	
28	Σ7	2, 4, 7, 14	GAIA Go
29	P		Bad
30		3, 5, 6, 10, 15	*Enochian Aethers* Ha
31	P		
32	2^5	2, 4, 8, 16	*Paths on the Tree of Life*
33		3, 11	*Degrees in Freemasonry*
34		2, 17	
35		5, 7	Add Face
36	6^2, Σ8	2, 3, 4, 6, 9, 12, 18	GEB
37	P		Dead
38		2, 19	KA Deed
39		3, 13	Deaf Odd
40		2, 4, 5, 8, 10, 20	
41	P		KIA
42		2, 3, 6, 7, 14, 21	AL
43	P		
44		2, 4, 11, 22	Ale
45	Σ9	3, 5, 9, 15	Dog God
46		2, 23	Food
47	P		HAD Loa
48		2, 3, 4, 6, 8, 12, 16, 24	OM An Egg Leo
49	7^2	7	Oil ABK
50		2, 5, 10, 25	*Sanskrit Letters* Good In
51		3, 17	AUM Ain Jade
52		2, 4, 13, 26	No

76		2, 4, 19, 38	Use
77		7, 11	TAO Eve
78	Σ12	2, 3, 6, 13, 39	*Tarot Cards* Bind Toe
79	P		Blood Rice
80		2, 4, 5, 8, 10, 16, 20, 40	Dance Debauch Kala Red
81	$9^2=3^4$	3, 9, 27	Rod
82		2, 41	KALI Abase
83	P		All Bat Cloud Fear
84		2, 3, 4, 6, 7, 12, 14, 21, 28, 42	IX
85		5, 17	LAM Cat Fire Sad
86		2, 43	LOKI Abate Gold
87		3, 29	MACHA Fur June Male
88		2, 4, 8, 11, 22, 44	Door Faerie Ox Seed Aids
89	P		Cave Hope
90		2, 3, 5, 6, 9, 10, 15, 18, 30, 45	
91	Σ13	7, 13	Cobra Cut Fat Man

92		2, 4, 23, 46	CIRCE Above Mana Web
93		3, 31	HERA Ages Amen Eye Line Mean Name Sage Taboo
94		2, 47	Alien Feet Four Hand Hair
95		5, 19	Bell Bow
96		2, 3, 4, 6, 8, 12, 16, 24, 32, 48	LUNA Alone Lion
97	P		Ash Five Gate Hero Lip
98		2, 7, 14, 49	AMUN Adder Agate Dread Luck Void
99		3, 9, 11, 33	Abbot Box Nine
100	10^2	2, 4, 5, 10, 20, 25, 50	Abacus By Fall Few Foot Grace Moon Opal

101	P		PAN Laugh None
102		2, 3, 6, 17, 34, 51	Afraid Fall The
103	P		SHU Because Black Child Fell
104		2, 4, 8, 13, 26, 52	Jet Kind Pain
105	Σ14	3, 5, 7, 15, 21, 35	Arm Behold Chance
106		2, 53	Flame Grief Noble Wood
107	P		Day MABON
108	$2^2 \times 3^3$	2, 3, 4, 6, 9, 12, 16, 18, 27, 36, 54	*Beads on a Mala* EPONA IMRA Drug Female Knife
109	P		DURGA Herd Union Wicca
110		2, 5, 10, 11, 22, 55	Fey King Heard Mind
111		3, 37	Final
112		2, 4, 7, 8, 14, 16, 28, 56	ORIEL Baby Break Bath Defeat Rain

113	P		SOL Guidance Hell Kite Who
114		2, 3, 6, 19, 38, 57	Abbey Angel Angle Demon
115		5, 23	Change Chaos Cheese Daemon Hidden Run
116		2, 4, 29, 58	HADES MAAT Dark Iron Rock
117		3, 9, 13, 39	BABALON Bridge Libra Queen Rune Sin Vale
118		2, 59	Amber Liber
119		7, 17	SEBEK Ant Blind Evil Hanged Live Son Time Veil Vile
120	5!, Σ15	2, 3, 4, 5, 6, 8, 10, 12, 15, 20, 24, 30, 40, 60	Abduct Death Magick Peacock Soul Ten

121	11^2	11	HADIT Coral Gemini Law Legion Love Nose Orion Rope Sun Tin Tome To me
122		2, 61	Anus
123		3, 41	Not
124		2, 4, 31, 62	IHVH Dream Fixed Lord Poor Value
125	5^3	5, 25	LUX Help Joy Note Owl Rare Touch Vine
126		2, 3, 6, 7, 9, 14, 18, 21, 42, 63	Burn
127	P		Axle Dagger Ordeal
128	2^7	2, 4, 8, 16, 32, 64	NUIT Eight Key
129		3, 43	Abandon Self
130		2, 5, 10, 13, 26, 65	ASAR MICHAEL Tomb
131	P		Wine
132		2. 3, 4, 6, 11, 12, 22, 33, 44, 66	ARIADNE Colour My Sand

133		7, 19	Art Circle Diamond May Music Not Rate
134		2, 67	MAYA Aries Ring
135		3, 5, 9, 15, 27, 45	EROS NOX Abyss Alcohol Green Rose
136	Σ16	2, 4, 8, 17, 34, 68	ANUBIS BRAHMA Animal Devil Healer Lived Phone Space Tree
137	P		Aether Cancer Rite Sigil
138		2, 3, 6, 23, 46, 69	Aqua Aura Ever Root Spice
139	P		Fault
140		2, 4, 5, 7, 10, 14, 20, 28, 35, 70	ADONIS ISIS SET Cups
141		3, 47	Dancer East Gloat Logos Magus Raw Sate War

142		2, 71	HEKATE GABRIEL Abundance Chakra Garlic Horn
143		11, 13	NEMAIN Qabalah Sound
144	12^2	2, 3, 4, 6, 8, 9, 12, 16, 18, 24, 48, 36, 72	CAILLEACH Calcite Chicken Flow Lady Wand Wolf
145		5, 29	Fight Khabs
146		2, 73	APOLLO LUCIFER Wind Order
147		3, 7, 21, 49	Caution Halite March
148		2, 4, 37, 74	Mask Moth Silk Vagina
149	P		Fly Freedom Group
150		2, 3, 5, 6, 10, 15, 25, 30, 50, 75	BAST Curse Ompehda
151	P		Bruise December Wicked Wise
152		2, 4, 8, 19, 38, 76	BEAST Desire Dharma Sex
153	Σ17	3, 9, 17, 51	JANUS Six Wheel Year

154		2, 7, 11, 14, 22, 77	PTAH Cover Dragon Ebony Heaven Obsidian Snake
155		5, 31	SAMAEL Finger Jewel Mouth Source Tongue Two Wave
156		2, 3, 4, 6, 12, 13, 26, 39, 78	Brow
157	P		Roman Say View
158		2, 79	CYBELE Crow Lung Pearl Yes
159		3, 53	April Marble
160		2, 4, 5, 8, 10, 16, 20, 32, 40, 80	Grave Tiger
161		7, 23	SELENE Cipher Limit
162		2, 3, 6, 9, 18, 27, 54, 81	Prime Strife Word
163	P		Cry Mason Fifteen Wax
164		2, 4, 41, 82	Earth Gates Grove Heart Holy Lips Will

165		3, 5, 11, 15, 33, 55	Amulet Ivy Lapis Sleep There Three Virgo
166		2, 83	Aether Ruby
167	P		Eleven Embody Emerald
168		2, 3, 4, 6, 7, 8, 12, 14, 21 24, 28, 42, 56, 84	Grow July October Ruby
169	13^2	13	HORUS SETH Legacy Way
170		2, 5, 10, 17, 34, 85	Haste Venom
171	Σ18	3, 9, 19, 57	FREY Number Plato Winged
172		2, 4, 43, 86	FREYA Ally Cyclic Honey Mars Penis
173	P		SHIVA ZEUS Health Night
174		2, 3, 6, 29, 58, 87	DUMUZI Jesus Fourfold ALGMOR
175		5, 7, 25, 35	Altar Woman
176		2, 4, 8, 11, 16, 22, 44, 88	August
177		3, 59	Indolence Staff

178		2, 89	LILITH Scourge Wish
179	P		Electrum Eighteen Light Prince South
180		2, 3, 4, 5, 6, 9, 10, 12, 15, 18, 20, 30, 36, 45, 60, 90	Many Shell Liver
181	P		Beauty Glamour
182		2, 7, 13, 14, 26, 91	Deity Lover Thebes
183		3, 61	PLUTO Chariot Father
184		2, 4, 8, 23, 46, 92	Prase Raven Ritual Spear Steam White
185		5, 37	Difference Rutile Volcano
186		2, 3, 6, 31, 62, 93	Lust Money
187		11, 17	Copper Saran
188		2, 4, 47, 94	RAPHAEL Shaman Valour
189		3, 7, 9, 21, 63	THELEMA Bliss Saint Total
190	Σ19	2, 5, 10, 19, 38, 95	URANUS
191	P		Disks Leaders Lotus Seven Thread
192		2, 3, 4, 6, 8, 12, 16, 24, 32, 48, 64, 96	Stone

193	P		Elixir
			Rowan
			Skull
			Sky
			Titan
194		2, 97	Andromeda
			Mary
195		3, 5, 13, 15, 39, 65	ABRAHADABRA
			IPSOS
			Infinite
			Orpheus
			Trance
			Witch
			Hither
			Kidney
196	16^2	2, 4, 7, 14, 28, 49, 98	HATHOR
			VENUS
			Centre
			Stop
197	P		Square
198		2, 3, 6, 9, 11, 18, 22, 33, 66, 99	Goddess
			Snow
199	P		
200		2, 4, 5, 8, 10, 20, 25, 40 50, 100	Citrine
			Cosmos
			Power
			Star
			Twin
201		3, 67	Rest
202		2, 101	Prudence
203		7, 29	AZOTH
			AZRAEL
			Pisces
			Stand
204		2, 3, 4, 6, 12, 17, 34, 51, 68, 102	HERMES
			Beryl
			Malachite
			Spell
205		5, 41	THOTH
			Crown
			Garnet
			Metal
206		2, 103	ASTERIA
			OSIRIS
			OSTARA
			Aquarius

207		3, 9, 23, 69	Flavour Flower Leather Rainbow Scorpio Sodalite
208		2, 4, 8, 13, 16, 26, 52, 104	SHAKTI Sirius Element
209		11, 19	Fluorite Hermit Horns Tarot
210	Σ20	2, 3, 5, 6, 7, 10, 14, 15, 21, 30, 35, 42, 70, 105	Knight Ordeal X
211	P		Cross Daughter Mother Precious Wands
212		2, 4, 53, 106	English Fortune Glorious Gnosis Peridot Spleen
213		3, 71	Children North Solomon Spinel
214		2, 107	VESTA Nataraja Fourteen Sphere Taurus Water Wisdom
215		5, 43	THEMIS Ammonite Jasper Throne Shekinah
216	6^3	2, 3, 4, 6, 8, 9, 12, 18, 36, 72	Carnelian Secret
217		7, 31	TEFNUT Powder Purple Vassago Eighty
218		2, 109	AIWASS

235		5, 47	Ivory Parent
236		2, 4, 59, 118	Success
237		3, 79	January Abomination Homeward
238		2, 7, 14, 17, 119	Egypt Lepidolite Throat
239	P		Truth Ultimate Blossom
240		2, 3, 4, 5, 6, 8, 10, 12, 15, 16, 20, 48, 60, 80, 120	Electrum Rhodonite
241	P		Celestial Phallus Warlock
242		2, 11, 22	APHRODITE Azurite
243	$9^3=3^6$	3, 9	Control Hexagram
244		2, 4	MORRIGAN VISHNU November
245		5, 7, 49	Cat's Eye Liberation
246		2, 3, 6	Solution Unveiling
247		13, 19	Silver Storm
248		2, 4, 8	ARTEMIS Zoisite
249		3	Lovers Matter Triangle Works
250		2, 5, 10	Elemental Kyanite
251	P		LASHTAL SEKHMET Company February Resolve
252		2, 3, 4, 6, 7, 9, 12, 14, 18	Tantra
253	Σ22	11	Connection Knowledge
254		2	Saturn

255		3, 5, 15, 17	KIALIAMIANIASIA
256	$16^2=4^4=2^8$	2, 4, 8, 16	Moldavite Scarlet
257	P		VITRIOL Capricorn Chalcedony Intuition Priest Tektite
258		2, 3, 6	Spirit Wizard
259		7	Atavism Desolation
260		2, 4, 5, 10, 13, 20	Meteorite
261		3, 9	
262		2	Current Sparkle Universe
263	P		Magnetite
264		2, 3, 4, 6, 8, 11, 12, 22	Kunzite
265		5	Misery
266		2, 7, 14, 19	
267		3, 89	Ancestor Psychic Stars Yellow
268		2, 4	Growth Twelve
269	P		Sapphire
270		2, 3, 5, 6, 9, 10, 15, 18	Amazonite Stairs Stands Yantra
271	P		DEMETER Warrior
272		2, 4, 8, 16, 17	Heliotrope Psalms Trident
273		3, 7, 13	
274		2	Labradorite Prophet Street
275		5, 11	Elements Harmony Sixteen
276	Σ23	2, 3, 4, 6, 12	MERCURY
277	P		

278		2	Sorrow Talisman
279		3, 9	Pyrite
280		2, 4, 5, 7, 8, 10, 14, 20	
281	P		Tourmaline
282		2, 3, 6	Gypsum Infinity Turquoise
283	P		
284		2, 4	Purity Stellar
285		3, 5, 15, 19	Starfire
286		2, 11, 13, 22	Staircase Thirteen Voltigeur
287		7	
288		2, 3, 4, 6, 8, 9, 12, 16, 18	Luxury Sweets
289	17^2	17	
290		2, 5, 10	
291		3	
292		2, 4	Moonstone
293	P		
294		2, 3, 6, 7, 14	
295		5	Christian Empress Temperance
296		2, 4, 8	CERNUNNOS Destiny Quartz Swords
297		3, 9, 11	
298		2	Sorcery
299		13	
300	Σ24	2, 3, 4, 5, 6, 10, 12, 15, 20	Splendour
301		7	METATRON Hierophant Mirrors
302		2	Information Pentagram Shatter
303		3	Serpent
304		2, 4, 8, 16, 19	Satiety
305		5	Exorcist Pregnant
306		2, 3, 6, 9, 17, 18	
307	P		
308		2, 4, 7, 11, 14, 22	SANDALPHON

309		3	RA-HOOR-KHUIT Pomegranate Key of it all
310		2, 5, 10	Twisted
311	P		Renaissance
312		2, 3, 4, 6, 8, 12, 13	September
313	P		Princess Sunstone Seventeen
314		2	Aventurine Television
315		3, 5, 7, 9, 15	Revolution Victory
316		2, 4	
317	P		Spectrum
318		2, 3, 6	Streaming
319		11	
320		2, 4, 5, 8, 10, 16, 20	Tigers Eye
321		3	
322		2, 7, 14	Happiness Instinct Servant Silver Bough
323		17, 19	
324	18^2	2, 3, 4, 6, 9, 12, 18	Swirling
325	$\Sigma25$	5, 13	Staurolite
326		2	
327		3	Sparrow
328		2, 4, 8	
329		7	Alexandrite
330		2, 3, 5, 6, 10, 11, 15, 22	Interference
331	P		
332		2, 4	
333		3, 9	
334		2	
335		5	
336		2, 3, 4, 6, 7, 8, 12, 14, 16	
337	P		Underworld
338		2, 13	Limitless
339		3	System
340		2, 4, 5, 10, 17, 20	Dark Energy Great Work
341		11	Marvellous
342		2, 3, 6, 9, 18, 19	
343	7^3	7	
344		2, 4, 8	
345		3, 5, 15	
346		2	

347	P		
348		2, 3, 4, 6, 12	
349	P		
350		2, 5, 7, 10, 14	Theosophy
351	Σ26	3, 9, 13	
352		2, 4, 8, 11, 16, 22	
353	P		
354		2, 3, 6	
355		5	Lapis Lazuli Serpentine
356		2, 4	
357		3, 7, 17	Adjustment
358		2	
359	P		Twenty
360		2, 3, 4, 5, 6, 8, 9, 10, 12, 15, 18, 20, 30, 36, 40, 45, 60, 72, 90, 120, 180	
361	19^2	19	Inspiration
362		2,	
363		3, 11	Oppression
364		2, 4, 7, 13, 14	Crossroads
365		5	Chrysocolla Dark Matter
366		2, 3, 6	
367	P		
368		2, 4, 8, 16	Rhodochrosite
369		3, 9	Electricity
370		2, 5, 10	Multiverse Sardonyx
371		7	Strength
372		2, 3, 4, 6, 12	Butterfly Exploration RPSTOVAL
373	P		Amethyst
374		2, 11, 17, 22	
375		3, 5, 15	
376		2, 4, 7, 8	Eternity
377		13	
378	Σ27	2, 3, 6, 7, 9, 14, 18	Restless
379	P		
380		2, 4, 5, 10, 19, 20	Manifestation
381		3	
382		2	
383	P		
384		2, 3, 4, 6, 8, 12, 16	Cruelty
385		5, 7, 11	
386		2	
387		3, 9	HOOR-PAAR-KRAAT

			NEPHTHYS
388		2, 4	
389	P		
390		2, 3, 5, 6, 10, 13, 15	
391		17	
392		2, 4, 7, 8, 14	
393		3	Priestess Transcend
394		2	
395		5	
396		2, 3, 4, 6, 9, 11, 12, 18, 22	
397	P		
398		2	
399		3, 7, 19	
400	20^2	2, 4, 5, 8, 10, 16, 20	Pythagoras
401	P		
402		2, 3, 6	Strangely
403		13, 31	
404		2, 4	
405		3, 5, 9, 15	
406	$\Sigma28$	2, 7, 14	
407		11, 37	
408		2, 3, 4, 6, 8, 12, 17	
409	P		
410		2, 5, 10	Understanding
411		3	
412		2, 4	
413		7, 59	
			Twenty-One
414		2, 3, 6, 9, 18	
415		5	
416		2, 4, 8, 13, 16	
417		3	
418		2, 11, 19, 22	
419	P		
420		2, 3, 4, 5, 6, 7, 10, 12, 14, 15, 20	
421	P		
422		2	
423		3, 9	
424		2, 4, 8	
425		5, 17	
426		2, 3, 6	
427		7, 61	
428		2, 4	
429		3, 11, 13	
430		2, 5, 10	
431	P		Rose Quartz

432		2, 3, 4, 6, 8, 9, 12, 16, 18	
433	P		
434		2, 7, 14	
435	Σ29	3, 5, 15	
436		2, 4	
437		19, 23	
438		2, 3, 6	
439	P		
440		2, 4, 5, 8, 10, 11, 20, 22	
441	21^2	3, 7, 9, 21	
442		2, 13, 17	
443	P		
444		2, 3, 4, 6, 12	
445		5	
446		2	
447		3	
448		2, 4, 7, 8, 14, 16	Chrysoprase
449	P		
450		2, 3, 5, 6, 9, 10, 15, 18	
468		2, 3, 4. 6. 9, 12, 13, 18	"This line drawn"
481		13	Rutile Quartz
508		2, 4	Do What Thou Wilt
514		2	Twenty-two
537		3	Smoky Quartz

Appendix 2 - Hebrew Alphabet Symbolism

Letter	Full	Eng.	Meaning	No	Esoteric Meanings
Aleph	ALPh	A	Ox	1	First Swirlings / Primal Energy / Air / Swastika / Manifestation
Beth	BITh	B	House	2	Void / Womb / Unconscious / Fertilization
Gimel	GML	G	Camel	3	Initiation / Transformation / Endurance
Daleth	DLTh	D	Door	4	Yoni / Cauldron / Chalice / Gateway / Oracle
He	HH	E, H	Window	5	Air / Visions / Divination / Pillars / Twin Goddess
Vau	VV	V, O, U	Nail	6	Phallus / Wand / Twin God
Zain	ZIN	Z	Sword	7	Lightning Flash / Intuition / Sword / Will / Personal Growth
Cheth	ChITh	Ch	Fence	8	Boundaries / Grail / Great Work / Oracle
Teth	TITh	T	Serpent	9	Wisdom / Sexuality / Kundalini / Union
Yod	YVD	I, J, Y	Hand	10	Hand / Sperm / Activity / Lovemaking
Kaph	KPh	K	Palm	20	Receptivity / Action
Lamed	LMD	L	Ox-Goad	30	Focus / Tools
Mem	MIM	M	Water	40	Water / Orgasm / Kalas / Great Mother
Nun	NVN	N	Fish	50	Primal Waters / Death / Menstrual Blood / Elixir Rubae
Samekh	SMK	S	Prop or Support	60	Ouroboros / Truth / Perseverance
Ayin	AyIN	Aa, O, NgH	Eye	70	Yoni / Third Eye / Sexual Union / Vision
Pe	PH	P, Ph	Mouth	80	Mouth / Tongue / Oracle/ Logos
Tzaddi	TzDI	Tz	Fish Hook	90	Boundary / Synthesis / Realisation through Sexual Activity
Qoph	QPh	Q	Back of Head	100	Pineal Gland / Moon / Sorcery / Astral / Oracle
Resh	RISh	R	Head	200	Head / Soul / Sun / Divine Wisdom / Autosexual Activity
Shin	ShIN	Sh	Tooth	300	Fire / Spirit / Triplicity / Circle / Elixir Vitae
Tav	ThV	Th	Cross	400	Earth / Balance of Elements / Void / Potential

David Rankine

Appendix 3 – Looking at The Path Attributions on the Tree of Life Glyph

Modern magick uses the attributions of Hebrew letters to paths given by the Hermetic Order of the Golden Dawn to the exclusion of any other system. While there is nothing wrong with this system, I include here two other attributions sets as well, to illustrate the point that we should never become so fixed in our practices that we are not open to revising or changing our perceptions if it is beneficial to do so.

If we look at the Sepher Yetzirah, then the attributions are given very differently. The earlier drawings of the Tree of Life glyph have some different paths on them to the version we use today, so we cannot make a direct comparison for this reason. It is interesting however to look at the patterns of attribution and their symmetry in the earliest glyphs.

The three mother letters (aleph, mem and shin) are on the three horizontal paths (14th, 19th and 27th). The seven double letters (beth, gimel, daleth, kaph, peh, resh and tau) are on the vertical paths (13th, 16th, 18th, 21st, 23rd, 25th and 32nd).

The twelve single letters (heh, vau, zain, cheth, teth, yod, lamed, nun, samekh, ayin, tzaddi and qoph) are on all the diagonal paths. This set of attributions has a natural inherent logic to it revolving around the geometry i.e. types of letters to direction.

A set of attributions I created based on ideas in the Sepher Yetzirah follows some similar ideas, but is also quite different. As in the Sepher Yetzirah, I have attributed the mother letters to the three cross paths, but in order of subtlety working down the tree. Thus aleph (air), then shin (fire), then mem (water).

The seven double letters I attributed to the seven paths which are totally above the abyss or run through the abyss. These double letters, with their planetary attributions, all fit very logically on the Tree in this manner.

Thus beth and daleth (Mercury and Venus) run from Kether to Chokmah and Binah, as a higher aspect of the Hod-Netzach polarity lower down the Tree. Likewise gimel with its lunar attribution as the 13th path going through Daath emphasises the Yesod-Daath mirror.

Resh (Sun) goes from the starry swirlings of Chokmah to the solar energy of Tiphereth. Kaph (Jupiter) is on the 16th path from Chokmah to Chesed (Jupiter). Peh (Mars) is on the 18th path from Binah to Geburah (Mars). Tau (Saturn) is on the 17th path from Binah (Saturn) to Tiphereth. As you can see every planetary letter attribution links in some manner to the planetary sphere.

The twelve single letters are then attributed to the remaining twelve paths on the Tree, forming the Wheel of the Year (Time) as a form of serpent ouroboros. This results in a radically different set of attributions, with only one of the twenty-two letters being attributed to the same path on the glyph.

Alternative Attributions

Path	Joins	Golden Dawn	Alternative
11	1-2	Aleph	Beth
12	1-3	Beth	Daleth
13	1-6	Gimel	Gimel
14	2-3	Daleth	Aleph
15	2-6	He	Resh
16	2-4	Vau	Kaph
17	3-6	Zain	Tau
18	3-5	Cheth	Peh
19	4-5	Teth	Shin
20	4-6	Yod	Qoph
21	4-7	Kaph	He
22	5-6	Lamed	Samekh
23	5-8	Mem	Nun
24	6-7	Nun	Ayin
25	6-9	Samekh	Yod
26	6-8	Ayin	Lamed
27	7-8	Peh	Mem
28	7-9	Tzaddi	Teth
29	7-10	Qoph	Cheth
30	8-9	Resh	Vau
31	8-10	Shin	Zain
32	9-10	Tau	Tzaddi

David Rankine

Appendix 4 -
Kala Attributions for Crystals

The following list of attributions is based on work I have done with crystals over the last 20 years, and you will find some of the attributions disagree with various books on the subject. All I can say is do what feels right.

Although certain materials like Amber and Jet are not actually crystals, it is convenient to include them as they are used in the same way. This list is not exhaustive, but I have tried to give all the common stones I could think of, sticking to their best-known names.

Agate: trigonal crystal, crystalline member of Quartz family.
Colour: green, blue, white, red, brown, yellow, orange.
Kala: Knowledge
Notes: protection whilst travelling, massage, healing of the body.

Alexandrite: rhombic crystal.
Colour: emerald green (red in artificial light).
Kala: Wind

Notes: used for eye problems, helps with clarity and insight.

Almandine: isomorphous cubic crystal, Garnet family.
Colour: deep red, violet red, black.
Kala: Blood
Notes: used for blood problems, and to produce resolve and determination to attain goals and complete cycles. May have four-rayed asterisms (stars).

Amber: natural resin hydrocarbon, amorphous.
Colour: yellow, reddish-brown, bluish, white, black.
Kala: Nature
Notes: a wonderful storer of charge and talisman. Good for general well being, a sort of psychic worry bead. Amber jewellery has become very popular in recent years, and so good amber is easy to find, though also costly.

Amethyst: trigonal crystal, Quartz.
Colour: violet.
Kala: Web
Notes: used for spiritual growth and protection, mental healing, purification. One of the prime magickal stones.

Aquamarine: hexagonal crystal, Beryl family.
Colour: sea green, sea blue.
Kala: Wave
Notes: good for relieving stress and emotional problems. Helps with psychism and clairvoyance.

Aventurine: trigonal crystal, Quartz.
Colour: green, brown, red or yellow with scales of mica.
Kala: Nature
Notes: used for skin complaints. Good for storing energy.

Bloodstone: trigonal crystal, crystalline member of Quartz family.
Colour: dark green with red spots.
Kala: Blood
Notes: strengthens the will and used with blood problems and protection from poison. Also known as Heliotrope.

Blue Calcite: trigonal crystal, Calcite family.
Colour: blue.
Kala: Wind
Notes: used for lung and voice problems, helps develop communication.

Carnelian: trigonal crystal, crystalline member of Quartz family.
Colour: translucent with white, blue or green colour.
Kala: Flame
Notes: helps with spinal problems, particularly lower spine. Good for clearing blocked sexual energy (works with the kundalini).

Chalcedony: trigonal crystal, crystalline member of Quartz family.
Colour: translucent with white, blue or green colour.
Kala: Wind
Notes: increases benevolence and reduces irritability.

Citrine: trigonal crystal, Quartz.
Colour: yellow.
Kala: Knowledge
Notes: helps maintain emotional stability in troubled times.

Coral: axial skeleton of the coral polyp, made largely of calcium carbonate.

Colour: red, pink, white, black.
Kala: Wave
Notes: for work with the bones, and to provide form to ideas. Coral has become more popular in recent times, and unfortunately is often obtained by using explosives to obtain the coral in quantity, thus destroying underwater ecosystems.

Crysocolla: hydrous copper silicate.
Colour: green, or greenish-blue with black.
Kala: Nature
Notes: good for storing energy, and for working with earth energies.

Crysoprase: trigonal crystal, crystalline member of Quartz family.
Colour: translucent apple green.
Kala: Wave
Notes: produces insight and hope.

Diamond: cubic crystal.
Colour: colourless, pale tints of yellow, red, pink, green, blue, brown.
Kala: Time
Notes: amplifies any energies, purifies. Diamonds will amplify negative energies as easily as positive ones, so if using diamonds, keep them and any other stones clean and well stored.

Emerald: hexagonal crystal, Beryl family.
Colour: grass green.
Kala: Love
Notes: good for healing, and for determining purity (including magickal purity). A good stone for magickal charge and seeing things clearly.

Fluorspar: cubic crystal.
Colour: violet, green, yellow, orange, blue, red, pink, brown, colourless.
Kala: Love
Notes: concerned with love, both physical and spiritual, and strongly connected with the heart chakra.

Haematite: trigonal crystal.
Colour: black
Kala: Blood
Notes: gives courage and endurance, used with blood problems and ulcers.

Iceland Spar: trigonal crystal, Calcite family.
Colour: colourless.
Kala: Wind
Notes: good for vision, both physical and astral, may be used with Ajna chakra.

Jadeite: monoclinic crystal.
Colour: green, pink, lilac, white, mauve, brown.
Kala: Nature
Notes: used for earthing and protection, good for kidney problems and "keeping your feet on the ground".

Jasper: trigonal crystal, impure micro-crystalline variety of Quartz.
Colour: reds, browns, greens, greyish-blue.
Kala: Blood
Notes: helps with liver and kidney problems, used to strengthen the physical senses.

Jet: fossilised wood.
Colour: black.

Kala: Time
Notes: absorbs negative energies like a sponge! Clean
regularly or you will pick up the negativity from it. A truly
lovely and magickal stone to use. Jet, like amber, has become
more popular and increasingly expensive; beware of French
Jet, which looks similar but is in fact coloured glass.

Labradorite: triclinic crystal, Feldspar family.
Colour: blue and grey, with play of colour.
Kala: Spirit
Notes: a stone for magickal growth and strengthening the
subtle body and mind.

Lapis Lazuli: mixture of minerals, mainly Lazurite and Calcite.
Colour: deep blue, often with golden specks of pyrites.
Kala: Devotion
Notes: for heart and spleen problems, symbolic of the cosmic
Goddess, and a good stone for magickal power, particularly
with the throat chakra and voicework.

Malachite: monoclinic crystal.
Colour: green.
Kala: Love
Notes: helps emotional problems and menstruation difficulties.

Marble: trigonal crystal, Calcite family.
Colour: colourless, white, grey with yellow, blue, red, brown
or black tints.
Kala: Ground
Notes: general earthing stone, helps maintain stability.

Moonstone: triclinic crystal, Feldspar family.
Colour: yellow or colourless with opalescence.
Kala: Sorcery

Notes: good for psychic problems, and for developing the psychic senses.

Nephrite: monoclinic crystal.
Colour: pale to dark green, white, black, brown.
Kala: Love
Notes: with Jadeite, these two stones are commonly known as "Jade". Use as Jadeite.

Obsidian: volcanic glass.
Colours: black, red and brown.
Kala: Time
Notes: perhaps the most efficient director of energy. Good for skrying and developing psychic powers. Also known as Apache Tears.

Onyx: trigonal crystal, crystalline member of Quartz family.
Colour: green, blue, white, red, brown, yellow, orange.
Kala: Ground
Notes: general healing, also circulatory problems and hearing difficulties. Used as a protection and grounding stone.

Orange Calcite: trigonal crystal, Calcite family.
Colour: orange, yellow.
Kala: Will
Notes: used for digestive problems, and to strengthen the emotions.

Opal: silica gel.
Colour: white (cacholong), semi-transparent orange to red (fire), transparent blue-white with red colour (girasol), colourless (hyalite), grey or brown (menilite or liver), yellowish or colourless with a play of colour (Mexican water), yellowish or bluish-white or white (milk), green (prase), yellow (resin).

The other forms are harlequin (regular size patches of colour), hydrophane (dehydrated, becomes opalescent in water), lechosos (shows green colour), moss (dendritic inclusions), matrix (showing some ironstone matrix), precious (showing good colour), white (pale ground), black (very dark ground).
Kala: Knowledge
Notes: used to help lung problems, promotes communication and mental growth.

Pearl: concretion of concentric layers of conchiolin (organic) and calcium carbonate around a small nucleus.
Colour: white, pink, black, bronze, gunmetal.
Kala: Tidal
Notes: helps with patience and resolution of outdated ideas and beliefs which need restructuring.

Peridot: rhombic crystal.
Colour: oil green, brown.
Kala: Nature
Notes: good for the digestive system. Helps with powers of analysis. Also known as Olivine.

Prase: trigonal crystal, Quartz.
Colour: green.
Kala: Wave
Notes: used for problems with water retention and urine problems.

Rhodochrosite: trigonal crystal.
Colour: rose red, may have shades of yellow or brown.
Kala: Love
Notes: directs energy, and is good for integrating different types of energy, such as physical, emotional and mental.

Rhodolite: isomorphous cubic crystal, Garnet family.
Colour: violet.
Kala: Web
Notes: used for lymph problems, and to strengthen the subtle body.

Rose Quartz: trigonal crystal, Quartz.
Colour: pink and white.
Kala: Love
Notes: used for promoting tranquillity and serenity, protection from negative emotions, emotional healing.

Ruby: trigonal corundum crystal.
Colour: red.
Kala: Blood
Notes: good for problems with blood and circulation, and for magickal strength. Both ruby and sapphire can have asterisms (six-rayed stars) and are hence known as Star ruby and Star sapphire.

Rutile Quartz: trigonal crystal, Quartz.
Colour: colourless with inclusions of rutile.
Kala: Tidal
Notes: used for the endocrine glands and bronchitis, also good for work with the ajna chakra. Also known as Needle Stone.

Sapphire: trigonal corundum crystal.
Colour: blue, colourless (white), yellow (golden), pink, green, purple, violet.
Kala: Devotion
Notes: good for mental problems, and developing mental discipline and willpower.

Smoky Quartz: trigonal crystal, Quartz.

Colour: transparent amber-brown.
Kala: Time
Notes: used for problems with kidneys, pancreas and sexual organs. Good protector and transformer of energies.

Sodalite: cubic complex silicate.
Colour: deep blue.
Kala: Devotion
Notes: general health and well being.

Sunstone: triclinic crystal, Feldspar family.
Colour: spangled bronze.
Kala: Will
Notes: good for general health and well being. Also known as orthoclase.

Tigers Eye: trigonal crystal, Quartz.
Colour: yellow or amber-brown chatoyant (cat's eye effect from refraction of light from fibres in the crystal), green chatoyant (Cat's Eye), blue chatoyant (Hawk's Eye).
Kala: Will
Notes: promotes clear self-perception and insight.

Topaz: rhombic crystal.
Colour: yellow, green, blue, pink (usually heat treated).
Kala: Will
Notes: promotes selflessness and purity of will, benevolence. A good stone for spiritual growth.

Tourmaline: trigonal complex boro-silicate.
Colour: colourless (achroite), red and pink (rubelite), green, blue, yellow-green, honey yellow, pale coloured (elbaite), violet (siberite), dark blue (indicolite), brown (dravite), black (schorl).

Kala: Web
Notes: good for dreamwork and spiritual growth. Promotes growth of the throat chakra.

Turquoise: triclinic phosphate of aluminium, copper and iron.
Colour: blue, green.
Kala: Devotion
Notes: used as a protection and charm, to absorb general negative energies.

Zircon: tetragonal crystal (high) or amorphous silicon dioxide and zirconium dioxide (low).
Colour: colourless, gold yellow, blue (all heat treated), honey yellow, light green, blue, red (high); leaf green to brown green (low).
Kala: Wind
Notes: used for liver problems, and gaining knowledge. Also known as jacinth.

Zoisite: rhombic crystal.
Colour: blue, green, yellow, pink, brown.
Kala: Love
Notes: for emotional problems and emotional growth.

David Rankine

Appendix 5
Classic Recipes

A lot of books talk about particular incenses and oils, but don't give them! I include here the classic recipes that are often left out, but that are very useful to have.

The oil and incense of Abra-Melin are both useful ingredients for ritual, especially for high energies and high aspirations.

Abra-Melin Oil

1 part	Myrrh	Add cinnamon to olive oil. Leave 1 week.
2 parts	Cinnamon	Add myrrh to mixture. Leave 3 weeks.
½ part	Galangal	Add galangal. Leave to mature. Strain.
1¾ parts	Olive Oil	

Incense of Abra - Melin

4 parts	Frankincense
1 part	Lignum Aloes
1 part	Red Storax

Over the centuries, much folklore has accrued around the legendary kyphi incense used by the ancient Egyptians. As this incense is often used by magicians I decided to include it here. There are various recipes available, the one I give here is the one I have blended from the ones I have seen, complete with instructions for making it.

Kyphi Ingredients

2 parts	Juniper Berries	½ part	Raisins
1 part	Red Sweet Wine	½ part	Gum Arabic
¼ part	Dragons Blood	2 parts	Galangal Root
½ part	Frankincense	1 part	Myrrh
1 part	Mastic	½ part	Benzoin
1 part	Honey	1 part	Broom Flowers
½ part	Opoponax	¼ part	Jasmine Oil
½ part	Lignum Aloes	½ part	Sandalwood Oil

How to Make It

Day	Mix 1 (Stored in Darkness)	Mix 2 (Stored in Sunlight)
1	Marinate the Juniper berries in the wine	
6		Grind Frankincense, Myrrh, Mastic and Benzoin finely together.
7	Add Raisins and mix.	
15	Grind the Gum Arabic down very fine and add to the Dragons Blood.	
16	Add the Dragons Blood and Gum Arabic to the marinated berries and raisins and blend well.	
21	Grind the Galangal root and add to the mix.	
22		Heat the honey so very liquid, add the mixed ground resins to it and the Broom flowers and blend together well.
29	Combine the two mixtures and add the finely ground opoponax, leave to blend in the dark.	
36	Add the jasmine oil, mix and leave to blend in the dark.	

43   Add the lignum aloes and sandalwood, blend and leave to mature in the dark.

56   Ready!

Bibliography

Note the suffix (M) indicates a magazine publication.

Barrett, Francis   The Magus or Celestial Intelligencer
I.G.O.S., California, 1998

Crowley, Aleister   The Book of the Law
Samuel Weiser Inc., Maine, 1976

The Goetia
Samuel Weiser Inc., Maine, 1995

Magick
Samuel Weiser Inc., Maine, 1997

Kaplan, Aryeh   Sefer Yetzirah: The Book of Creation
Samuel Weiser Inc., Maine, 1997

Grant, Kenneth   Cults of the Shadow
Frederick Muller Ltd, London, 1974

David Rankine

|---|---|
Grof, Stanislav	The Adventure of Self-Discovery SUNY Press, New York, 1988
James, E.O.	The Ancient Gods Phoenix Giant, London, 1960
Mathers, S.L. MacGregor	The Book of the Sacred Magic of Abramelin theMage Dover Publications, New York, 1975
Pinch, Geraldine	Magic in Ancient Egypt British Museum Press, London, 1994
Rankine, David	A New Analysis of IAO Dragon's Brew No. 12 (M)

Crystals – Healing & Folklore
Capall Bann Publishing, Somerset,
2002

The Prime Qabalah
Chaos International No. 25 (M)

Sex Magick & The Kalas
Dragon's Brew No. 12 (M)

writing as
Jack Dracula

Creative Crystallomancy
Chaos International No. 13 (M)

Feeding the Soulfire
Stone Temple No. 5 (M)

Kundalini Rising

Dragon's Brew No. 17 (M)

Making Misery Magickal
Chaos International No. 17 (M)

Making Mutable Mantras
Chaos International No. 11 (M)

The 9 Gates & The Magick Sphere
Stone Temple No. 1 (M)

Weaving Wyrd Webs
Chaos International No. 10 (M)

Rankine, David
& Rainbird, Ariadne   Magick Without Peers
Capall Bann Publishing, Somerset,
1997

Tigunait, Pandit R.   Sakti: The Power in Tantra
The Himalayan Institute Press,
Pasadena, 1998

Von Bingen,
Hildegard   Physica
Healing Arts Press, Vermont, 1998

White, David Gordon   Kiss of the Yogini
University of Chicago Press, Chicago,
2003

Wilkinson, Richard H.   Symbol & Magic in Egyptian Art
Thames & Hudson, New York, 1994

David Rankine

The Complete Gods and Goddesses
of Ancient Egypt
Thames & Hudson, London, 2003

Woodroffe, Sir John   The Serpent Power
Ganesh & Company, Madras, 2003

Recommended Reading

Rather than recommending a long list of specific books, I include here details of the authors who have had the most impact on my development and learning.

Carlos Castaneda – whether his material was genuine or the work of a brilliant charlatan, for me the important fact is that Castaneda presented ideas of personal development and ethics which will continue to inspire people for a long time to come. He has certainly inspired me through my life.

Aleister Crowley – the man responsible for most of the occult renaissance of our time. Apart from his seminal work "Magick", which started me on my path at age 14, as the receptor of Liber Al, the greatest magickal grimoire of recent centuries, Crowley will always have a place in my list of greats.

Mircea Eliade – the French anthropologist. Eliade's work draws together a huge range of ideas and material, presenting an immense amount of valuable source material and ideas for the magician.

Kenneth Grant – one of the few magicians of the last century to actually present new and inspirational ideas and material, and look at the dark aspects of magick. Kenneth Grant is the man who inspired me to develop my system of magick.

Stanislav Grof – one of the pioneers of consciousness research, Grof presents a fascinating insight into concepts of perception and consciousness which I have found invaluable.

Wilhelm Reich – Freud's other great pupil apart from Jung. Reich was that rare phenomenon – a Renaissance man with a genius that spanned a whole range of fields. Reich's work on the body and sexual energy are especially valuable to study.

Austin Osman Spare – the brilliant magickal artist. Spare's ideas and artwork, and the techniques he created, have been some of the most influential in the last century of magick.

Index

Mandrake

'Books you don't see everyday'

Fries/*Cauldron of the Gods: a manual of Celtic Magick.* **552pp, royal octavo, 186992861x £24.99$45 paper (£40/$75 hardback special)**

Fries/*Seidways Shaking, Swaying and Serpent Mysteries.* 350pp 1869928-369 £12.99/$25
Still the definitive and much sought after study of magical trance and possession techniques.

Fries/*Helrunar - a manual of rune magick.* 454pp 1869928385 pbk, £14.99/$30 Over 130 illustrations. new enlarged and improved edition
'...eminently practical and certainly breaks new ground.' - Ronald Hutton

Fries/*Visual Magick: a manual of freestyle shamanism.* 196pp 1869928-571 £10.99/$20. '*A practical modern grimoire.*' The Cauldron

Vayne/*Now Thats What I Call Chaos Magick.* 198pp, 1869928741 pbk, £12.99/$25

Steven Ashe/*Qabalah of 50 Gates.* ISBN 1869928-237, £10.99/$20

Harris/*Witcha: a book of cunning* isbn 1869928776 £12.99/$25

Channing/*Chaos Hieroglyphica.* 200pp, 1869928830. £14.99/$30. special hardback

David Rankine

Wilson/*I, Crowley - Last Confession of the Beast 666 - Almost*
£9.99/$20 250 pages ISBN 1869928 547, second edition
'*Brilliant . . . the Great Beast explaining himself in lapel-grabbing prose:*' Simon Callow,

Rigakis/*Threskia: traditions of the Greek mysteries.*
1869928 660, 250pp, £12.99/$25

Morgan/*Thelemic Magick I.* ISBN 1869928342, 90pp, £9.99/$18

Morgan/*Medicine of the Gods: Basic principles of Ayurvedic Medicine* 100pp. 1869928091 £10/$18 .
.trustworthy . . . intellectually challenging, Rahul Peter Das in Traditional South Asian Medicine

Dukes/*What I did On My Holidays - Essays on Black Magic, Satanism and Devil Worship.* ISBN 1869928520 £18/$35 - 420pp.

Smith/*The Books of the Beast.* ISBN 1869928172, 128pp, £9.99/$19.99 pbk

Bryant/*Merlin's Mound*, ISBN 1869928768, 198pp. $6.99/$14. Young adult fiction. "a wonderful book...in the same category as Alan Garner and Susan Cooper"
Professor Ronald Hutton

Order direct from
Mandrake of Oxford
PO Box 250, Oxford, OX1 1AP (UK)
Phone: 01865 243671
(for credit card sales)

UK price includes surface post worldwide
online at - www.mandrake.uk.net
Email: mandrake@mandrake.uk.net